PRAISE FOR SILENT SORORITY

Winner of the 2010 Team RESOLVE™ Choice Best Book Award

"A Top 10 Indie Book to Read this Spring 2010." *–More.com*

"Mother's Day looks different from where she stands."
— Lisa Belkin, *The New York Times*

"Witty, fun, heartbreaking, and absolutely bittersweet."
— Marcie Pickelsimer, *Grown In My Heart*

"...a tour de force, a rare jewel. This is a memoir of a clearly intelligent woman. *Silent Sorority* is without a doubt a landmark book"
—M.C. Prinsloo, *In Vivo*

"*Silent Sorority* does a great job addressing the invisibility of non-Moms."
— Christina Gombar, *More.com*

"If you are battling infertility or have a friend or family member who wants or needs to try to understand how infertility changes *everything*, I recommend Pamela's book."
—Laurie Gordon, Executive Editor, *Fertility Authority*

"*Silent Sorority* is a brave book and a gift to all infertile women, whatever stage of the journey they may be on."
— Kate Johnson, *NBC/iVillage*

Silent Sorority

A (Barren) Woman Gets Busy, Angry, Lost and Found

A Memoir
Pamela Mahoney Tsigdinos

This book is dedicated to all
who have struggled to find a new path.

---

*"There is no experience from which you can't
learn something. When you stop learning you
stop living in any vital and meaningful sense.
And the purpose of life, after all, is to live it,
to taste experience to the utmost, to reach out eagerly
and without fear for newer and richer experience."*

– Eleanor Roosevelt

CONTENTS

INTRODUCTION

Imagine learning that your body is incapable of ever conceiving a child. There will be no fruit of your loins. One instant you are like everyone else. The next, you're not. Your DNA now ends with you.

You are infertile.

Your branch of the family tree will forever be just a truncated twig. You've been denied a rite of passage, a biological imperative. You had no say in the matter. It wasn't a conscious choice. The comfortable sense of continuity and legacy others take for granted disappears in an instant.

Take a moment to really think about it. What are you supposed to do? How do you feel? Is there a particular way you're supposed to feel? I mean, really, how do you prepare for that?

Okay, now get on with your life. You know, have a nice day.

Infertility is a touchy subject. It's supremely personal, involves sex organs, and is one of the last arenas where it is fair game to heap scorn. That's because conventional wisdom today leads many to believe that infertility is self-inflicted, or a byproduct of feminism gone bad — ergo it's okay to withhold any sort of compassion or show of interest.

In social psychologist Melvin Lerner's book, *The Belief in a Just World: A Fundamental Delusion,* he argues that people want to believe in inherent justice, and that people who appear to be suffering are in fact responsible for their own situations. According to the "just world" hypothesis, society has a strong desire or need to believe that the world is an orderly, predictable, and just place, where people get what they deserve.

Funny thing though. I have yet to meet or come across anyone who *deserved* infertility, and I've come to know quite a few women (and men) of all ages, ethnicities, religions and political views who have had to confront the condition. Those in my silent sorority are far from a homogeneous group.

What I can tell you about my sisters and me is that we freely donate our time and dollars to causes that help children in particular and society in general. We pay our taxes. We vote. We recycle and we worry about global warming. We cry when tragedies strikes. We laugh at the absurdities life serves up far too often. We love life. We are in awe when we experience nature at its finest.

The primal urge to create is a powerful one. In my case, there were several times when we were in our 30s that my husband and I resolved to accept that our bodies were simply incapable of conceiving a child. We did our best to be rational, to not let emotions or primal longings dictate our life. We were, after all, supposed to be "evolved," right?

We looked at the statistics. We debated the trade-offs. We decided that the world didn't really *need* a little Pammie or an Alex Junior. We dedicated our naps to friends who were fighting sleep deprivation from long nights with colicky babies. We tried to reassure each other, with a smattering of superiority, that we were more than our fertility. That worked for several months at a stretch. Then the urge to reproduce would come back larger than before, propelling us forward with the next medical treatment, the next in a line of what almost felt like hokey-pokey-esque routines aimed at getting our cells to commingle.

I'm still waiting to overhear a couple on the verge of starting a family who enthusiastically say, *Let's* not *try using the old fashioned way. Whaddya say we go the high tech route? It'll be great! Let's give a few of the local hospitals and fertility clinics a whirl. You know I've always wanted to have my private bits examined at length by people in white coats. And those hormones injected with the long needles? What's more romantic than that!? Won't it be great to spend thousands of dollars on treatments not covered by our medical insurance, with no guarantees? What ARE we waiting for?*

Ours was a decade-long struggle to have children. Even I was amazed at how far I was willing to go. The risks to my health I was willing to take. The desire to conceive, rational or not, was *that* strong. Even if you haven't personally suffered with infertility there's a very strong likelihood that your sister, your daughter, your granddaughter, your friend, your neighbor, your colleague or the woman standing next to you in the grocery store has.

Taming biology is not quite as simple as many think. I challenge some of the nearly billion parents on the planet who have reproduced to turn back the clock and shut off that part of their brain stem – turn off that sex drive, too. (They are apparently related.) As evolved as we claim to be, Mother Nature still exercises some serious power over us. Convoluting the matter, baby-making gets wrapped up in political or religious arguments. Somehow our society has lost sight of the fact that outside of the arm waving and pontificating about the negative impacts of feminism and who controls reproductive rights, a slice of the population (12 to 14 percent) face a very personal sadness.

At its core, infertility involves two individuals who love each other and yet cannot joyfully, spontaneously conceive. But there's more. In the wake of conception failure, I've discovered that as hard as the loss of pregnancy and "normalcy" was, making a life in the long shadow of infertility has its own unique challenges. With the stigma and judgment surrounding this difficult human experience, it's not surprising that many choose not to speak about it. The silence, though, can be deafening and defeating.

SECTION I:
HAPPILY EVER AFTER
TAKES A FEW LEFT TURNS

CHAPTER ONE

EPIPHANY IN
THE LADIES ROOM

As far as ladies rooms go, the one I was hiding in some two years ago wasn't half bad. Actually, it was quite cheerful. Bold colors, purple and orange, brightly surrounded me as I fretted and contemplated my next move. Just outside the door a Napa Valley bistro hummed with happy patrons sampling their *amuse-bouches* and homey French cuisine. Normally I'd want to be on that side of the door savoring the wine, soaking up the cozy atmosphere and inhaling the delectable aromas wafting out of the bustling kitchen. Not that night though. That night I wanted to transport myself anywhere but back to the table where my colleagues were effusively riffing on their children.

There are only so many things you can do in a ladies room to kill time, but at that moment anything was preferable to waiting for my entrée with a fake smile frozen carefully in place, all but invisible to those at my table. As I studied my unmasked face in the mirror, a frown took shape. I looked more tired at that moment than I should. Maybe I needed to change facial moisturizers? And what about those skin tightening claims I had bought hopefully from Macy's aisles of beauty? From the looks of my softening jaw line, they clearly weren't living up to their promise.

My once-bright eyes were awash in sadness, but not because of the few wrinkles and sags. No, I had a bigger problem weighing on me. There was no amount of makeup that could camouflage the emotion and anxiety that raged in my heart and my head. What a contrast *that* was to the carefree (bordering on self-important) "aren't we just the best parents ever?" chit-chat that precipitated my escape. It was hardly the first time I'd run for cover to avoid the pain that such bonding inflicted. In fact, ducking out of that kind of "normal" adult chatter had become far too familiar a routine. Do you have any idea how often baby- or child-rearing talk is the central topic of conversation? Let me put it this way: I was running out of places to hide. What worried me more than a little was that I wasn't sure if my escape/avoidance thing was just a phase or a permanent, troubling way of life.

Fast approaching my mid-40s, I had once imagined, by that point in my life, I would be right in there trading stories with colleagues, friends and family about the joys and frustrations of parenting. I'd have 2.5 pre-teen kids and a really messy laundry room. I should have been worrying about whether we'd have enough money set aside to pay for college tuition. Oh, yeah, and I was supposed to be having a love-hate relationship with a minivan (love, love, love its functionality but hate what it does to my image!). Our over-sized house should be somewhere in the suburbs, close enough to good schools, decent jobs and a mega-mall or two, but far enough away from anything really interesting like quirky shops, ethnic restaurants or museums. According to the script I should be following, I'd be torn between how much time I spend at my job and how well I'm parenting my kids.

Except that wasn't my life. And it had taken me a while to accept that it never would be. Did I really want to spend my Saturday mornings at soccer games complaining with other parents about the need for the latest school fundraiser? Was there some magic to fighting with kids about why they needed to put the Wii down and get started once and for all with their homework assignments?

On paper that life didn't sound all that exciting. So what gives? Why did I somehow feel big chunks of my life were missing? How was it that I found myself in the ladies room trying to reconcile, again, that I'd never live the life of a frazzled but seriously proud suburban soccer mom, complete with my very own mommy blog?

More importantly, why did I go silent or hide at social events? How did I lose my voice in the first place? What happened to my identity? Who the hell am I?

———————⬥———————

I am no saint.

But that didn't stop my father from referring to me that way one spring in the late 1970s. As in, "Ah, Saint Pam is home. How was this afternoon's visit with the old folks?"

It was nearing the end of my sophomore year in high school, the spring I spent as a candy striper at a local nursing home. I never could figure out how refilling water pitchers, plumping pillows, or talking to frail, blue-haired women who wanted to touch my soft, unlined face qualified me for sainthood, but I did know that those Thursday afternoons after school walking the halls of that drab two-story building smelling of urine exhausted me more than the cross-country runs required other afternoons at track practice.

What drove me to volunteer? Well, at the awkward age of nearly sixteen I was intent on building a resume that would make me look appealing to a prospective university. There were no ifs ands or buts about it – I was going to college. It was simply a question of which one, and I had my eye on the University of Michigan. In addition to top grades the college admissions staff wanted a well-rounded incoming freshman class. Community involvement was one way to highlight that I was a self-starter, an industrious member of society. I had the time. After-school jobs in 1978 were hard to come by with the economy in Detroit bumping along the bottom. One of the biggest employers in the area, Chrysler Corporation, was facing bankruptcy for the *first* time.

The collapse of an automaker was only background noise to me since my father didn't work in the auto industry. You could tell by the condition of the rusty, eight-year-old car in the driveway that my dad was a writer. He had dreams of one day publishing a novel but instead was covering the newly formed Department of Energy for *The Air Conditioning, Heating and Refrigeration News*. When he wasn't writing editorials about chlorofluorocarbons – long before it was hip to discuss global warming – he would patiently edit my English papers. The topics ranged from current events like the status of the Equal Rights Amendment to a sci-fi-sounding new "test tube baby" born that year in England. He never cut me any slack with his copy editing and my writing improved greatly as a result. When he wasn't explaining the evils of dangling participles, my father encouraged me to read Evelyn Waugh's *Brideshead Revisited* and F. Scott Fitzgerald's *The Great Gatsby* among other modern-day classics.

Now lest you think I was heartless, volunteering at a nursing home simply to build my resume to compete in what Walter Cronkite each night warned was fast becoming a global economy, I did get a warm rush seeing the wrinkled faces light up when I arrived on the scene for a chat, especially from those who had no children. And there was a deeper motive behind my efforts to get ahead.

"You don't want to end up like me," my Grandmother Stella would regularly whisper to me, starting when I was no older than ten. "Don't ever rely on a man to provide for you. You need to provide for yourself. Remember this: Make sure you can be independent."

Standing on skinny legs in slacks that never seemed to be long enough, I'd nod solemnly. It wasn't hard to understand why she felt that way. Our whispering in her small kitchen surrounded by pots of fragrant boiling cabbage and sauerkraut would inevitably elicit a barking inquiry from the next room. My wheezing grandfather nursing emphysema and poor circulation from the comfort of a large La-Z-Boy chair was a suspicious man. Ever the conspiracy theorist, it was only a matter of time before he would bellow, "What are you talking about out there? I can't hear you!"

Our hushed conversations would end as quickly as they began. Meanwhile Grandma Stella would roll her eyes and bring him a cold beer or some other pacifier to avoid a Mount Vesuvius-like temper tantrum – curious and more than a little scary to watch coming from a man approaching 65.

Apparently the bellowing had begun not long after he married Grandma Stella. When they met she was a slender, alluring, starry-eyed blonde – totally defenseless when it came to men in tuxedos. She was one of fourteen children born to Polish Catholic immigrants. Let me repeat that because it's highly relevant to my story – she was one of fourteen (!!) children. No fertility issues there. Raised in the shadows of the Allegheny Mountains in the coal mining town of Scranton, Pennsylvania, Stella's life was not her own. She was either working behind the counter of her parent's small grocery store or taking care of one of her younger siblings. She had dreams of a better life, though, and they came in the form of something tall, dark and handsome.

During the day, Grandpa lived underground in the coal mines. He'd surface grimy and black at the end of his shift. He must have used excessive amounts of soap because from the looks of photos framed on the wall he cleaned up quite nicely. He had to. He spent his evenings, often in a white tuxedo, seated on a stage in a smoky club. He was part of a swinging jazz band and was equally comfortable wailing on a saxophone or a clarinet.

Here we had a young Polish Catholic man who loved to make music and a sheltered Polish Catholic dame who loved to dance. A marriage made in heaven? Sadly, no. She tried unsuccessfully to leave him just weeks after they married. That her face was black and blue didn't persuade her old-country parents to take her back. She was married now and more importantly, Catholics *didn't* divorce. Her desperation for freedom led her to escape briefly two more times during their nearly 50-year marriage. I say briefly, because with no marketable skills, two daughters and no driver's license, she was in no position to throw her hat in the air and turn the world on with her smile. At a tender age I learned there had to be a better way to live a life than under the thumb of a domineering man. Until the day she passed on Grandma Stella never let me forget that.

So, okay – growing up with super-sized feet, buck teeth encased in braces, a flat chest and toothpick legs I didn't have any problem fighting off the boys. That I wasn't on their radar screen didn't bother me much. I was going to be independent after all. I devoted my time to more erudite matters, graduating from the Laura Ingalls Wilder collection to *Anne of Green Gables* to Jane Austen's finest. There was a common denominator there: spunky, fearless girls or women.

Meanwhile, my parents were raising four kids in a comfortable but unpretentious Detroit suburb where the trees were relatively new and the houses were well-built but not overly large. Our first house was just four miles north of the legendary Eight Mile Road. When I was ten years old my family moved to a slightly larger house on the edge of a more affluent suburb where the residents measured other people's worth by designer clothing, square footage and country club memberships. We didn't have any of the above on my dad's modest salary but we did have, among other things, a boisterous family of six that gathered every evening at 5:30 p.m. for dinner, our annual summer vacation "up north," and regular trips to the library.

Unlike my grandparents, my parents had just about the happiest marriage on the planet – equal say in all matters, a true partnership. From day one these two went together like fish and chips, which we ate regularly on Friday nights during Lent. They met at the *Varsity News*, he the editorial director and she the society editor across the newsroom on the campus of the University of Detroit. My mother had designs on the Big Apple, including aspirations in publishing. That was before my father swept her off her feet. Just shy of ten months after they married, my older brother arrived. I was born eighteen months later, followed by my sister fifteen months after that. Just under two years later, my baby sister came along.

Growing up, it was hard to miss the steady and passionate voice of Helen Reddy on the radio belting out, "*I am woman, hear me roar / in numbers too big to ignore.*" It was an exciting time to be a girl, with all kinds of talk about breaking glass ceilings and going where no women had ever gone before. The classified ads in newspapers went from Help Wanted *Men* and Help Wanted *Women* to just Help Wanted. I was "Free to Be" whatever or whoever I wanted to be. Marlo Thomas and Mary Tyler Moore were having the time of their lives.

Meanwhile, each Sunday my family filled a pew. On the second Sunday in May the Catholic pageantry took on even greater significance. As the light streamed through the stained glass windows in the small chapel it radiated a rainbow of colors onto the stone floor. The illumination seemed to skip along the worn wood as music rose from the organ in the balcony. The priest would begin his slow walk up the aisle to the altar while the moving melody of "Ave Maria" filled the space. This was the day in May that honored Mary and all mothers. It would begin like every Mother's Day mass I could recall. The priest would first welcome the parishioners and single out his mother, who was always seated in the first pew. He would then motion to one of the altar boys to gather up a bouquet of red roses, and proceed to extol the virtues of motherhood and the sacrifices that these selfless women had made on behalf of their children. Then, with a dramatic flourish, he would grab a single red rose and ask for the newest mother to make herself known.

"Who has delivered a child in the past month?" he would ask. If he saw more than one hand go up he would shorten the time horizon. "The last three weeks? The last two?" Inevitably there would be what looked like a newly released patient from a maternity ward who would make a point of attending the Mother's Day mass solely to earn the honor of being the one who had most recently come out of the delivery room.

Next, the priest would offer rose tributes to the oldest mother, the youngest mother, the mother with the most children, the grandmother who had the most grandchildren, and just to mix it up a bit, the mother who had traveled the farthest to join her children that day. Each rose recipient held her head high and seemed to nearly burst with pride at her maternal accomplishments. I dreamed of the day when I might take possession of a rose. Yes, I wanted my chance to be in the winner's circle at this makeshift Roman Catholic "Breeder's Cup."

I was convinced I could have it all and then some, but there were some reminders that it might also be harder than it looked. In our living room one evening, I crouched on the steps out of sight and eavesdropped on an unusual gathering of women. They had arrived for what I thought was called a "Wrap Session." Of course, I had mistakenly assumed they'd be wrapping gifts of some kind. Instead they were there to "rap" – not sing, but consciousness-raise. What it devolved to, though, was comparing notes about the mostly boring lives they were leading and how having kids too early cramped their style or held them back from realizing their dreams. This life thing was starting to look a bit complicated.

Even in my most insecure moments my dad had made me believe I was the most beautiful, courageous, smart daughter a father could ever want. And that took some imagination on his part. I had been born with what one doctor described as "undeveloped eye muscles" that left me looking cross-eyed for a time. Fortunately for me my blue eyes did settle into place, right about the time my parents discovered I was pigeon-toed. The leg braces my parents took turns strapping me into at night during my toddler years did their job straightening me out. I could run like the wind when I was five.

It was bike riding that had me more than a little unnerved. My father had sweet-talked me into giving it my best shot after watching me sit on my new bike in the driveway while my siblings rode up and down the street. His advice about moving the pedals backwards to brake and stop didn't quite sink in. With what must have been comical frequency I panicked with each run going full speed into a cement parking block and flying over the handlebars or careening across the pebble-peppered asphalt sideways. After each fall my father would gently pick me up, dry my tears, calm my fears and coax me back onto my banana seat, running behind me until I finally mastered my balance and the brakes and could ride without assistance.

On hot, humid summer nights he would sit on the patio, the smoke from his cigar keeping the mosquitoes at bay. Once "The Brady Bunch" and "The Partridge Family" TV shows had ended and it had grown dark, I could see where my father was, based on his cigar's glowing orange ember.

"Pambo," he would call out. "Come outside and talk to me."

Sometimes the invitation for me to prattle on was aimed at taking his mind off weighty matters like Watergate; other times it was to hear and test my opinions. A product of a Jesuit education, an English major, my father relished ideas, reasoning, and the beauty of language. He told me life was a smorgasbord, and I should sample all it had to offer. Together with my mother, my father taught me to love learning and expression. They both encouraged me to reach as high as my dreams could take me, celebrating every victory, no matter how small.

Like many late-blooming girls, I found the social aspects of high school lacking. Those years offered up the usual self-esteem hard knocks. A lowlight was my embarrassingly uncoordinated and, not surprisingly, unsuccessful tryout for the pom-pom squad. Why subject myself to such nonsense? My mother had been a cheerleader, so I felt it was my duty to carry on the tradition. Needless to say, my failure to make the squad led me to distance myself from comparable *uber*-girl activities including, later in college, the sorority rush set. I found other ways to emulate my mother, like excelling in school. (My mother had skipped a few grades and graduated at the top of her class at sixteen.) My defeat at something as inane as pom-pom tryouts taught me that if I couldn't play the cute card and run with beauty queen crowd I could always succeed on my wits.

By the end of my senior year in high school my world began to turn Technicolor. I smiled more than I had in years since my orthodontist had removed the railroad-track braces imprisoning my teeth. So long, headgear. Like Dorothy opening the door into the Land of Oz, I saw a magical world awaiting me. No matter that no boy saw fit to invite me to the Senior Prom – I was going to the University of Michigan. My colt-like figure still acquiring grace, my father knew my ego could bruise like a peach. He conferred with my mother and together they came up with a plan. He told me boys my age were incapable of fully appreciating my charms and invited me to join him on a business trip to Washington, D.C. on what would have been prom weekend. Distracted by visits to the Smithsonian, the White House and other must-see national monuments, it was easy to forget what was taking place without me around the school grounds and in the gymnasium.

On the night of what would have been the big dance, I felt infinitely cooler than the chicks back in the Detroit area parading around in taffeta and lace and getting endlessly pricked by corsage pins. I pulled a stylish hot pink jersey dress onto a slim but increasingly curvy body that seemed to change by the day. I felt the weight of the dress hug and hang in all the right places. I stepped into strappy sandals and brushed on some blush and mascara, all the makeup I wore in those taut skin days. If the male heads turning in my direction and the eyes following me approvingly in the restaurant were any indication, I had transformed from an ugly duckling to something approaching a swan.

My father had made reservations at a trendy Georgetown restaurant. I sipped on my first glass of wine. We talked history and politics while a jazz band played in the background. I felt infinitely more important than any silly old Prom Queen. To this day I don't regret missing out on that teenage milestone because that D.C. trip made me realize that a dance is just a dance, but having a devoted father who helps make happy memories is something you keep close to your heart your whole life through.

That wasn't the only thing I'd learned about life so far. Like my mother, I developed a penchant for making lists. I was becoming something of a control freak, and lists were one way of keeping things, well, under control. On my teenage to-do list:

- STEER CLEAR OF MARRIAGE WHERE THERE'S NO POWER-SHARING AGREEMENT.

- THE WORLD IS MY OYSTER. I CAN GROW UP TO BE ANYTHING I WANT TO BE (AND, ACCORDING TO THE TV SHOWS OF THAT DAY, WEAR GROOVY BOOTS AND MOD OUTFITS).

- DON'T CONFUSE "FITTING IN" WITH BEING SUCCESSFUL.

- BE AWARE THAT KIDS ARE A BIG RESPONSIBILITY SO MAKE SURE YOU'RE READY FOR THEM.

Also in my teenage years I honed my mothering skills by babysitting other people's children for the princely sum of fifty cents an hour. A veritable pro at wiping noses, overseeing disputes and getting kids bathed and to bed, by college I had a different sort of nurturing test. It came during a semester when I volunteered in the preemie unit at the University of Michigan hospital. A friend and I worked the late shift once a week as part of a developmental child psychology class. Our responsibilities were minimal – but given the environment – daunting nonetheless. In one dimly lit and ever so hushed corner of the hospital, cartoon animals cavorted on the walls and mobiles hung from the ceiling. During each visit we tried to bring tender care to the most diminutive of patients. They lay in tightly wrapped bundles, their delicate scrunched-up faces under the smallest caps imaginable. We held and softly rocked those preemies big enough to come out of their islets. For the tiniest ones intricately hooked to an array of softly humming monitors we could do very little other than simply share soft, encouraging whispers or alert the nurses if anything looked amiss. With each passing week we cheered for the little souls who fought to stay warm, thrive and grow to their 40-week term.

By the time I wrapped up college there was something new to consider. The "biological clock" thing had become all the rage. It was ominous and ever-present. Seems I couldn't pick up a newspaper or magazine without reading about it. More stuff for the growing list.

- Don't forget that women's eggs have a time limit. *Check.*

- Graduate from the University of Michigan. *Check.*

- Get my budding career in corporate communications on track. *Check.*

Where to from there? Well, it would be disingenuous to leave out a chapter of my life but since it now feels like a million years ago, I'll be brief. I surrendered without much of a fight to the "everyone's doing it so I need to do it" wedding frenzy. You had to be there to understand just how powerful the bride mystique was. And it was compounded by religious canon dictating, in so many words, that I would go to Hell if I lived with a man who was not my husband. The result: I inadvertently repeated the same error my grandmother did settling down with the first guy who fit the minimum criteria to wear a tux and join me at the altar.

I'd been off campus four years, but my college boyfriend was still in my life. We'd broken up more than once, which should have been a clear sign that we weren't right for each other, but I couldn't see beyond the stars in my eyes and the desire to be part of the "bride tribe." It makes me cringe now to acknowledge how easily I fell for the happily-ever-after myth. My wedding day was fairy-tale-like. There was a grand ceremony worthy of a girl from fine Catholic stock. On an unseasonably warm Indian summer day I wore a wedding gown complete with a train that could best be described as a Lady Diana-wannabe. She had captured the world's interest with her wedding at Westminster Abbey just a few years earlier. Like many other bedazzled girls, I set my alarm clock for 5 a.m. to watch the ceremony live.

Now it was my turn. I even had my own picturesque stone chapel renowned for its ecclesiastical architecture as the backdrop. In an ironic twist I made my entrance from the church crypt. While the guests ar- rived above and listened to a string quartet I was below in an ominous, medieval-esque environment that included a statue of St. Joan of Arc. I jumped from the Middle Ages and landed at the evening wedding recep- tion in what felt more like the 1920s, complete with a serenade from my newly-betrothed's fraternity brothers. I returned to the modern era after our honeymoon. I figured my new mate and I would work hard at our jobs, make babies and reward ourselves with a week or two of summer vacation with our brood somewhere in northern Michigan. We would frolic on the sandy beaches of the mighty Lake Michigan and pile up our beach toys and umbrella in a humble cottage on or near Grand Traverse Bay or outside of Petoskey. That's just the way it was done.

It wasn't too long before my new husband and I began trying, first with joyful expectation and then curiously without success, to start a family. We lived just eleven miles from my parents and the church where I had made my first confession. I had been happily making headway in my budding career, but well into my twenty-ninth year I was also eager to add a new dimension to my life and follow the familiar script, you know – the one calling for me to join the "mother tribe"– but the *working* mother set. The M.R.S. Degree, marry-young-and-then-retire types, not only gave me the heebie-jeebies, they confounded me. Why a woman nearly twenty years after the women's movement began would *willingly* lose herself so completely in a one-dimensional, economically dependent role struck me as both weak and unwise. Grandma Stella's indentured servant experience had been seared into my consciousness. I could all but hear her warning: *don't make the same mistake I did.*

I was wholly convinced that my inability to conceive in my prime child-bearing years was driven by my husband's fertility-dampening case of adolescent mumps, though we never learned for certain what the impediment was. That's because in the process of building an expensive new house we started bickering about more than the light fixtures. We were suddenly at odds about the type of *life* we wanted to build. Was this a man I could spend the rest of my life with? I tried to submerge my doubts but they only returned in my subconsciousness. In one vivid and anxiety-riddled dream, a nightmare really, I was lying in a hospital bed in a delivery room, well into a painful labor. The doctor told me my husband was outside. I panicked. I suddenly did not want to continue with the delivery. I realized, awakening in a fright, that this man was not who I wanted as the father of my children. The obvious next question: Why was I married to him then? Our relationship had deteriorated beyond repair. Our views were no longer aligned – though I wondered if they ever had been. We were clearly moving down two different paths. We were destined to make each other miserable.

Unlike my grandmother, I not only recognized I had made a bad decision about my choice of mate, I was willing to correct it even if there was a high price to pay. While I would miss the pageantry of the Catholic Church (and lose my good standing with this influential institution), excommunication was not enough of a deterrent. If the tradeoff was a lifetime of unhappiness – its own form of Hell – or the *threat* of going to Hell, I'd take the latter. Not long after my disturbing dream I initiated divorce. To say it was difficult would be a supreme understatement. Among the hardest conversations in a series of tough acknowledgements was the one with my doting but very dutiful parents.

It was April, the week before Easter. I showed up unexpectedly on my parents' porch and knocked on the front door, careful to avoid a wreath decorated with festively colored eggs. Surprised and delighted, my mother welcomed me in. Her expression changed to concern when I mumbled that I had something important to share, and a favor to ask. Out of the corner of my eye I could see fresh palms tucked behind a crucifix hanging in the hallway. I hung my head and sighed. I wanted to know, I said slowly, if I could move back home – just temporarily. My mother gasped. She wanted to know if it was serious or just a bad misunderstanding. She tried to reassure me, explaining that all marriages have problems.

Attempts at counseling had only affirmed that my relationship was irreparably broken. No. I wanted a divorce. I sat on the sofa shivering uncontrollably waiting for my tradition-bound father to come home while my mother made tea and tried to make sense of my upsetting news. Above the baby grand piano opposite where I sat was a picture of my family in more innocent times. There I was, happily surrounded by my older brother, younger sisters and parents. I wore a chocolate-brown velour top, a plaid skirt and an innocent grin locked in braces. We sat casually arrayed amid colorful leaves in a Birmingham park – the epitome of the all-American family.

I jumped when the door rattled. In walked my father who announced in a sing-song voice as he always did, "I'mmm hoooome." A smile broke across his face when he saw me sitting in the living room.

"Pambo! What a lovely surprise."

My mother reappeared with a worried, pinched look on her face. "Pam has something she needs to tell you."

"What is it, baby?"

That's when I lost it. After nearly six years of trying to stay married I had failed my parents and myself. All I could choke out as he reached over to embrace me in a hug was, "I'm sorry. I'm so, so sorry."

My divorce not only devastated my parents, it challenged my sense of judgment and left me something of a pariah amid my more happily married friends and colleagues. It also pushed back any plans to start a family while baby announcements started arriving in droves. The first thing I did after a judge declared my divorce final in December 1995 was march down the hall of the courthouse and arrange to take my name back. I realized how important my given name, my identity and my ability to direct my life were to me.

It was also time to revisit and update, where necessary, my earlier formed beliefs:

- Steer clear of marriage where there's no power-sharing agreement *and make sure your mate is compatible.*

- The world is my oyster. I can grow up to be anything I want to be. **Still true**.

- Don't confuse "fitting in" with being successful. **Still true**.

- Be aware that kids are a big responsibility so make sure you're ready for them. **Still true**.

———

Some six months after my divorce and at 32 years old I made plans to leave the Detroit area. I was ready for a new lease on life. I set my sights on a future in California – and not just any old part of California, but the epicenter of creation: Silicon Valley. I wouldn't be alone. My older brother was now living in the area and from my honeymoon I had taken away an unusual souvenir, a California-based friend. On opposite sides of the country on the same day – she in the San Francisco Bay area and me in a northern suburb of Detroit – we had each walked down the aisle. She and I had hit it off immediately on the deck of the Star Princess Cruise ship basking in the sun and in our honeymooner status. Even with a brother and pal on hand to help, I was more than a little nervous about what awaited me in the Golden State. I had secured a position in marketing at a computer company in San Jose.

In the weeks leading up to my move over Memorial Day weekend 1996, my mother struggled to find words of advice. Since her dream of going to New York hadn't materialized, my relocation to California seemed somehow more daunting. Over a lunch of grilled cheese and tuna sandwiches, with a hint of sadness in her voice, she said, "This is so unlike anything I ever imagined for you. Sure, you had opportunities I didn't have with a career and all, but I guess I always thought your life would be more like mine -- marriage, kids…"

I looked at her sheepishly. "So did I."

"You're a smart, resourceful girl but you do have a tendency to trust a little too easily. Be careful. Don't let anyone take advantage of you."

On the eve of my departure with my bags all packed and ready to go Grandma Stella was there to wish me well. Despite a growing dementia that caused her to get confused, she was sharp as a tack and supportive when I needed her to be. She never chastised me for my divorce.

"Grandma, I'm going to California tomorrow."

"What's that dear?"

"I'm moving to California."

"Well, that's good, honey. You know variety is the spice of life."

As usual, she was right. California offered everything I had been missing in Michigan. In addition to the much kinder climate, there was a healthy disregard for the status quo, an enthusiasm for pushing in new directions. Failure was accepted as nothing more than a step that moved one closer to success. You don't like your job? There's something better waiting around the corner. Just head over to a Hobee's restaurant where every morning you'd find one or more wild-haired geeks pitching an idea to a risk-loving investor over coffee cake. On every corner it seemed a newfangled coffee café called Starbucks was opening and lining up to buy three-dollar cups of fancy coffee were people of every imaginable ethnicity. I eagerly embraced the zeitgeist. Casual Friday become casual Monday. Pinball machines and ping pong tables filled common areas.

Volleyball games in the office complex courtyard became the new staff meeting. I moved from one company to another before I'd had a chance to fully unpack all the boxes I'd brought from Detroit.

Within my first year in the Bay area I bought a house with Alex, a man I had fallen for deeply, passionately. He was an executive speechwriter when we first met. His tall, powerfully-built physique wasn't lost on me but his eyes were what sealed it for me. They twinkled with mischief and delight. He was quick to laugh and could find humor in most any situation – like the time I wasn't feeling well after something in a rich meal didn't agree with me. I told him I needed to get home – that I was feeling a bit, well, nauseous.

"I have that affect on women," he said apologetically.

I didn't know whether to laugh or hurl.

When Alex had been born in Boston there were only 48 states, and the president was an old guy named Dwight Eisenhower. Alex and the president had one big thing in common. They both loved Jeeps. I don't know about Dwight, but Alex had a penchant for naming his Jeeps: Little Shirl, Big Shirl, Grand Shirl. You might detect a theme here. Shirley was his mother's name. The tie-in? The first Jeep he bought, a Wrangler, was fire-engine red. Its vibrant color reminded him of his mother's mop of curly auburn hair.

In time I learned that Alex had shouldered a number of heavy personal burdens, all before he turned 30. He was the baby of the family, the youngest of three children. A week before he was born Shirley was making arrangements for his then five-year-old sister, Deb, to become a ward of the state of Massachusetts. The job of caring for a mentally retarded daughter, a newborn, and a rambunctious toddler was too much for Shirley to handle.

Alex's older sister had experienced complications during her birth but their impact wasn't immediately obvious. It was only when Shirley's second child, a boy, started to crawl, that it became evident Deb had severe developmental problems. In 1958 there were few options for special needs kids. Sadly, institutionalizing children like Deb was the norm.

Shirley made sure Alex and his brother knew their sister nonetheless and instilled in them a sense of responsibility to look after those less fortunate. Shirley was a no-nonsense nurse who worked night shifts so she could spend time after school with her boys. During the summer months she took nursing assignments at a sprawling camp. Her sons slept in spartan cabins or in sleeping bags under the stars. There, they could hike, swim and learn archery, among other wilderness adventures.

On the afternoon of Good Friday when Alex was just seven he saw his best friend killed in a tragic accident. His little pal ran into the street just as a pickup truck zoomed around a curve. Good Friday forever became Sad Friday. He still paid respects at his friend's grave years later when he stopped by the cemetery to visit his mother's grave site. His beloved mother – the woman who had once baked homemade gingerbread to construct into elaborate houses during the holidays – had passed away suddenly when Alex was in college. Heart failure.

Ten years later, Alex would visit his terminally ill father, grabbing a flight from San Francisco to Detroit at the end of each third week of grad school to be with him over the weekend. He offered to quit school to be there full-time. His father, a Greek immigrant who had gone on to get his Ph.D. in chemistry, would hear none of that. "Finish school," was his reply. While Alex sat helplessly at his father's bedside, Alex heard him say, "You've always been a good boy." This was the ultimate approval from a man who didn't talk much or demonstrate affection easily.

Alex lost his father to cancer on the eve of his thirtieth birthday and willingly signed on to become his sister's guardian. He later joined the board of the non-profit organization that managed the group home where Deb lived. He took calls in the wee hours of the morning when the east coast-based staff forgot about the three-hour time zone difference. Though Deb couldn't form words, the staff said her eyes lit up and she would smile broadly when hearing that her little brother was coming for a visit. Alex would sit beside her, hold her hand and tell her stories. Sometimes they went to restaurants or on shopping trips, despite the fact some people would point fingers and stare. "She has just as much right to enjoy a sandwich – albeit not as neatly – as *they* do," he'd say.

It took a lot to rattle Alex's cage. I adored him for his cool, calm presence. His low-key demeanor and dry sense of humor kept me from taking myself too seriously. When I'd reluctantly acknowledge a foible, he would say with mock seriousness, "Pammie, my work with you is almost complete." If he was a stable atom, I was the free radical. I pushed him out of his comfort zone and he kept me from spinning out of orbit.

Gun-shy on the whole marriage thing, I was perfectly happy to just be a couple. Alex and I lived in sin, but we did so in the nicest possible way. We shared a love of history, literature and the University of Michigan Wolverines, all of which we discussed regularly during our commute to work together up the peninsula on Highway 101. Alex took great joy in playfully baiting me. He could eloquently debate both sides of an issue, which meant I was usually left stammering, not sure whether he was serious or looking to highlight a flaw in my rationale. In many ways Alex reminded me of my father. Both knew just the right way to challenge me, delighting in my spunky, sometimes naive bravado, with a mixture of curiosity and care.

Alex was also a man-child. Introduce a ball and he became ten years old all over again. He liked to hit them, kick them and throw them. He was also pretty good at fixing things, and that was convenient because I was really good at breaking things. His nickname for me was "Pamdemonium." Alex indulged me and celebrated my idiosyncrasies. He never complained about my cooking, though some meals deserved it. He cut a mean lawn and a fine figure. He could load and unload a dishwasher with the precision of a surgeon. He surprised me with his laundry skills and taught me the finer points of fire-building and popcorn making – the old fashioned way with oil and kernels. He killed spiders for me and let me warm my cold feet on his side of the bed. I wanted to bear his children for reasons that went far beyond accepting a rose in the Roman Catholic Breeders Cup. I knew unequivocally that he was the man I wanted and trusted to be beside me in the delivery room and through the challenging days of parenting.

Not long after I arrived in California, my brother, a free spirit who had spent a few years traveling the world before settling down, became a first-time father. What he said about seeing his daughter Madeline for the first time was tender and unforgettable. "If I had known I could feel love as intensely as this, I wouldn't have waited so long to be a father."

The deep affection and caring my brother showed his daughter was aw-inspiring. "Aw, look how he cuddles her." "Aw, look how worried he gets when she sneezes." "Aw, he even changes diapers?"

His fierce devotion to Maddie went beyond anything I could have imagined. He had always been a good-hearted, sweet-natured and dutiful big brother but his transformation to father revealed a new dimension I found altogether endearing. Nothing was more important now than his daughter's well-being, safety and happiness.

My niece stole my heart, too. I visited Maddie whenever I could. I simply adored her. Even with my solid babysitting foundation I still harbored fears that I'd break her somehow. When called upon to babysit, I peppered her mom and dad for pointers before they left me for an afternoon commitment. I still remember our first night together — just the two of us. Through the baby monitor I heard stirring most of the night in the room next door. It was an altogether new, anxiety-producing sound. I was convinced Maddie would wake up in a fright, aware that her parents were gone. But it was I who was fitful. I didn't sleep but a few hours. With each awakening I strained to hear what was going on in the room next door. Her soft breathing on the monitor reassured and allowed me to fall back asleep.

When the stirring sounds continued at 6 a.m., I tiptoed down the hall and carefully opened the door to find Maddie in her crib twirling her blanket with the most innocent, curious gaze one could imagine. The door squeaked when I opened it further announcing my arrival. Maddie turned her head toward the doorway. I could see my brother's quizzical expression on her face. After a moment, she smiled in recognition and eagerly reached her arms up to be held. After a diaper change I scooped her up and carried her down the hall to my bedroom. Maddie tucked herself onto my hip for the ride and snuggled her head onto my chest. Once on the bed with me she scampered in her footie pajamas over a pillow to reach for her favorite picture books – the ones we had studied so happily the night before. Maddie returned and enveloped herself in my presence.

"Lelephant," she announced in a husky, sleepy but serious voice. "Yes, elephant," I answered, pulling her closer into the crook of my arm. That sweet, simple experience was seared into my mind. The bond, the trust, the connection was intense. I relished my role as make-believe mother and reveled in the warmth of my niece's little body in her soft cotton PJs. I felt her heartbeat and breathing quicken as she enthusiastically recognized and pointed out animals and various other shapes on the pages. In that moment, Maddie could not have been more content. And neither could I.

There was no doubt in my mind. I was 33 and wanted to be a mother in my own right. Equally important, Alex – whom I lived with but was not married to – welcomed the idea of fatherhood.

"Expand the tribe? I'm game," he said. "Hey, do you want to get started now? I can't *wait* to see how you handle being barefoot and pregnant."

Persona non grata as far as the Catholic Church was concerned, I allowed myself to color outside the lines. Further, the official ceremony to certify the legitimacy of my first union hadn't worked out so well. Bye-bye birth control.

Like many women on the path to motherhood, I started nesting and collecting adorable baby outfits in anticipation. It seemed the smart thing to do. Collect the outfits and various gear over an extended period of time so that it wasn't a big expense all at once. I even started clipping diapers coupons for future use. I shopped for baby shower gifts with a new sense of fascination and wondered what my baby registry would look like. Now at the top of my latest to-do list:

- Stock up on at-home pregnancy tests. *Check.*

- Wait for pregnancy...

- Wait for pregnancy...

- Wait for pregnancy...

Negative? Negative?! NEGATIVE??!!

Hey, hold on. Wasn't getting pregnant supposed to be as easy as getting too familiar with the opposite sex? Alex and I knew each other really, really well – and often – in the biblical sense. So, why was it I kept flunking the pregnancy tests? What could it possibly be? My eggs were grade A. I was in great shape. I ate green leafy vegetables. I exercised. I drank lots of water. I paid my taxes on time. And this had to be good for bonus points: I had led an effort to raise money for the March of Dimes.

CHAPTER TWO

DISBELIEF: I CAN'T BE INFERTILE, I'M CATHOLIC, FOR PETE'S SAKE

Disbelief bordering on alarm set in after a year of "trying" without success. There's nothing quite so humbling or perplexing as finding out that your body has failed you. What to do when it refuses to play by the rules? Well, if you're like most people you try to find out why. Some couples and their ailments are easier to fix than others.

When I first started down the path of doctor visits I was convinced all I needed was a pill. Isn't that what we've all been socialized to believe? I didn't fully appreciate while I was looking for a quick fix that an army of reproductive endocrinologists had been mobilizing since 1978 in the wake of Louise Joy Brown's debut as the first in vitro fertilization – or test tube baby – success story. Since first throwing open the doors to their fertility clinics, doctors in towns and cities across the world had all but minted money. Fertility decoding had spawned a $3 billion industry. Who paid attention to such things? Clearly not me.

After a while, getting knocked up became all-consuming – practically the only thing I could think about. Every possible contributor to my mysteriously barren body became suspect. (*Was it the Pop Tarts I ate as a kid? Maybe that OFF mosquito repellent? That stuff was evil smelling.*) I put my research skills to work. There were no books too cumbersome, no magazine or journal article too obscure. Many of the library books I found on the topic of reproduction were already checked out – this was pre-Dr. Google, mind you, when people still relied on libraries as a primary form of information search. It seemed those having trouble making babies devoured everything they could get their hands on.

And so it began. One instant I was like everyone else. The next I wasn't. My poor DNA. It felt so rejected. It wanted to know what it did wrong. And Alex's DNA? It ruled and it too, felt the blow. After all, Alex's DNA had led to a University of Michigan German literature major who went on to become a naval officer who served in a peacekeeping mission in Beirut before earning an MBA. His mother could trace her heritage back to the Daughters of the American Revolution. And now? Now our branch of the family tree was in jeopardy

Amateur that I was, when I wanted some answers on the baby-making front I naively sought out a baby doctor, an ob/gyn. I was convinced that someone trained in obstetrics was the place to start since they had expertise *delivering* lots of babies and all. I looked in my company's healthcare directory and found a doctor who had only recently set up practice. We'll call her Dr. Newbie.

I cut to the chase during my appointment and told her we'd been doing our bit to try to increase the population of California – but without any luck. Before I could say anything further she yelled out "Clomid." I thought for a minute she was yelling for her assistant to join us.

"Clomid. It's a fertility drug." She clarified as she reached for her med school text book. "Now what's the proper dosage?"

Ah yes, I nodded. "CLOMID. Isn't that the weirdly powerful drug best known for causing women to throw litters of children?"

While Dr. Newbie wrote out the prescription, my mind filled with magazine covers – not of your traditional reed-thin cover girls but of curiosities who became the subject of voyeuristic night-time news shows because they conceived and delivered multiple babies at once.

Dr. Newbie looked up from her textbook. "Don't worry. It's just a pill."

Ah, yes, a pill. That's what I was there for.

"It's typically the first fertility drug offered," Dr. Newbie went on. "Instead of one egg, multiple eggs get released in a cycle. Look at it as improving your odds. If more than one egg gets loose, well, you increase your likelihood of getting pregnant."

This was gambling in a very strange new way. I wanted one, okay, maybe two babies in any given nine months' time – Alex's father had been a fraternal twin – but clearly with Clomid a basketball starting team could result. I felt queasy and I wasn't even anywhere close to being pregnant yet. After returning from the pharmacy with my prescription, I pulled out the drug materials the pharmacist had included. It instructed me to start taking a tablet on the fifth day of my cycle and continue taking the tablets for five days. What I really wanted to know about were the side effects:

> "Clomid may cause hot flashes due to changes in
> hormone levels. Occasionally, abnormal ovarian enlarge-
> ment with symptoms of abdominal discomfort and/or
> pain can occur. Other adverse reactions include breast
> tenderness, headache, nervousness, dizziness, nausea and
> vomiting, fatigue and temporary visual disturbances."

Ah, yikes. This new-found relationship with Clomid suddenly seemed too risky to trust to a newbie physician. Clearly this wasn't, forgive the pun, child's play. Before I undertook risking my otherwise healthy body for the privilege of cranking out a few more eggs, I decided I needed a second opinion.

I reached for the other brochures I'd found in the doctor's office. One was ever so cheerfully titled "Infertility: Causes and Treatments." It left me cold. Could there be any more damning descriptor? Synonyms tumbled through my mind: barren, harsh, inhospitable and incapable of bearing fruit. It suddenly dawned on me that my womb might actually be broken, damaged, or simply useless. Taking a deep breath I opened the brochure and read the first few paragraphs.

> "Couples are considered infertile if they have not been
> able to conceive after 12 months of having sex without

birth control. More than one factor may cause infertility. Some are easily diagnosed and treated, others are
not. In some cases, no cause can be found. About 14%
of couples in the United States are infertile."

Fourteen percent!? That number was much higher than I would have
guessed. That was hardly encouraging, but what surprised me further was
the description of the odds for perfectly functioning women at the peak of
fertility. Apparently even for those in their early to mid-twenties, the odds
were only twenty percent that they could conceive during any one cycle.

Short of a chastity belt, I, and most girls I knew, had been terrorized
into believing that the conventional sex act would automatically lead to
a baby on board. With odds at just twenty percent, either there was a lot
of hanky-panky going on or some people were incredibly lucky – or not,
depending on their point of view.

Those were the days when each fact I came across was new and mind-
blowing. Now I'm practically a licensed fertility clinician. You want to
talk personal knowledge about how things operate? I can all but give
you a blow-by-blow of where my egg is at any given point – from the
fallopian tube to the tip of the uterus. My plumbing familiarity, unfortunately, made not one iota of difference. Meanwhile, everyone around
me glowed. Had the whole flipping world suddenly gotten pregnant?
Let's see. There was the next-door neighbor, the office receptionist, the
ladies in front of and behind me in the grocery store, the sister-in-law,
the stray cat and the goldfish. Me? I had nothing going on with the *ute*
but a monthly reminder of failure. No amount of lighting candles and
prayer seemed to change the outcome. My stork was seriously lost. I was
starting to lose my mind. I had one-sided conversations with my body as
I studied it carefully in the mirror.

*What gives, bod? I've taken great care of you – all six feet of you. I am
a big believer in preventative medicine. I try not to eat too many evil carbs.
Aren't those vitamins doing something other than making the water in the
toilet bowl turn a fluorescent yellow-green?*

The doctor raised the question of my uterus. What do you mean, my uterus might have something wrong with it? Nobody ever said anything about any *young* uterus problems. *Old* uterus problems, sure, who doesn't know all about that tick-tock thing? So, just what is going on here? Do I need to remind you that my great-grandmother cranked out fourteen babies? My mother was no slouch either. For Pete's sake, I'm Catholic. *Okay, not in good standing, but still.* I can't possibly be – what's that horrible, ugly word? Infertile? Ick! No, don't say it again. I don't want to hear it. That's not me. Really. Check it out. All the parts are there. I donate regularly to Goodwill and to food drives. I volunteer on our neighborhood association board and help organize community events. I plant trees near vacant lots. I grow flowers and the occasional pumpkin patch. There. You see? A green thumb. Isn't that worth something? Can we work with that? *No?*

I'd always been one to read and follow health guidelines. I was an insurance company's dream – *especially* since none of the treatments for problems in the fertility department were covered. Yeah, that was an added kick in the head.

So what were some of the more intriguing things I learned in my early attempts at treating infertility? There was the usual stuff, like: remember to have sex and lots of it. *Got that covered.* Stay out of hot tubs. *A bit of a challenge – we live in California after all – but not insurmountable.* Choose boxers over briefs and cut out the caffeine and booze. Nothing too drastic there compared to the days of yore when people appeased the gods of fertility by killing goats and chickens to make sacrifices. I'd seen more than my fair share of blood – every twenty-eight days to be exact – best to leave that technique to the ancients.

But in defense of the ancients they weren't as out there with their bizarre, stoke the baby-making process as we might think. We modern types aren't that much better. For instance, ice cream. Yes. Ice cream. Apparently a diet rich in ice cream and other high-fat dairy foods could lower the risk of one type of infertility, according to a Nurse's Health Study at the Harvard School of Public Health. And if diet tips were what you were after, there was so much more! Avoid donuts – too many trans fats. Increase the green leafy vegetables. The same Nurse's Health Study researchers published fertility diet guidelines widely touted by mainstream newsmagazines and infotainment shows.

Why did I get the feeling that with each new "how-to" out there we infertile folk were going to get our share of unsolicited but well-meaning advice from friends, family and colleagues about how to get a bun in the oven. *You can do it in just ten easy steps! Seriously, I read about it in* Good Housekeeping *or was that* Cosmo? *Anyway ten steps – you gotta try it!*

What I didn't want in those early days of discovery, what repulsed me to the core, was the idea of becoming a full-blown human science experiment – where conception occurred *outside* our bedroom. A pill like Clomid, while it had its obvious downsides, wouldn't interfere with our sex life. We could still rely on candlelight and a little help from the likes of soulful singer Al Green to set the mood. Any talk of Petri dishes made me squirm. Creatures throughout the food chain had mastered the primal dance. Surely we would get to the finish line ourselves without going to ultra-extreme measures.

In the meantime, my adopted home, Silicon Valley, had reached a frenzied state. It was 1998 and Internet mania had led to the birth (see, I can't get those conception metaphors out of my head) of hundreds of startups. During the heady dot-com days, tech companies were poaching each other's employees and adding new levels of employee benefits to keep those on board from jumping ship. Since I was stressed out wondering how long it might take us to get pregnant I fell, not surprisingly, for the edict in many women's magazines that confidently recommended "relaxing" as a critical pregnancy contributor. I was all for it. I indulged in the latest new company perk, a twenty-minute massage made available onsite in a conference room for $20. While this diversion offered a temporary relaxation opp, it did nothing for my uterus.

I did my best to pretend that everything was just fine. *We'll get this figured out. No need to get alarmed. Come on, we're in Silicon Valley – the place where all things are possible.* I immersed myself in projects at work. There was plenty to distract me, what with visitors from around the world dropping by to see how the cradle of innovation operated. One particular guest had me completely star struck. Princess Diana's father-in-law, HRH Prince Philip, Duke of Edinburgh and the Queen's consort, was in town to raise awareness for one of his charities. I was among those who organized a tour and lunch in his honor. After hearing one of our technical types describe how security software operated, HRH charmingly observed, "I have no idea what you just said, but it all sounds very important. Thank you very much."

It was the lighter moments at work that kept me from going completely nuts. But after more negatives results on the repro front, it was clear I had to overcome my aversion to Petri dishes – time to forego the candlelight and romance scenario I had long envisioned would lead to pregnancy. It all seemed so old-fashioned – quaint really – get familiar with your mate and, tra la, nine months later a baby would arrive.

Alex and I had a series of mind-numbingly boring and unsatisfying discussions with specialists about FSH levels, scrotum temperatures, sperm morphology and ovarian reserve. We underwent scary and painful exploratory tests and surgeries to get a better understanding about why we weren't conceiving naturally. I'll spare you the gory details about the time I passed out after my first laparoscopy or the painkillers needed to dull the excruciating, sharp jabs that erupted somewhere deep in my lower abdomen region every time I moved or took a deep breath. I will give you only the highlights.

It had been a couple of years since we decided to let nature take its course. It was in the fall after I turned thirty-five when the full battery of diagnostic test results came in. Little did we know when we started that Mother Nature had seemingly lost her bearing. Alex and I found out that our genes looked great on paper (our DNA *really* liked hearing that), but our cells needed some extra help to commingle and go the distance. Early on, when things were taking longer than expected, we jokingly wondered if we should take up smoking or recreational drugs, quit our jobs and apply for welfare. From the looks of it, that seemed a sure-fire way to get knocked up. While not scientific, judging from what I'd seen in my life, taking a less responsible approach to parenting had seemed to work really well for quite a few other people.

Unfortunately we learned it wouldn't be quite that straightforward. We had some *bona fide* medical conditions. I had endometriosis, a condition marked by uncontrolled tissue growth in the uterus. I had the lesions surgically removed, and the doctors sent me home with every expectation that I would have no further trouble conceiving. Alex had a condition called varicocele, an enlargement of the veins in the scrotum that lowers sperm count and quality. Not a deal breaker by any stretch, but odds of conception apparently would be much higher if we relied on experts to wash and select the best looking sperm.

While it was a long shot that even the most carefully timed sex would lead us to pregnancy, we weren't prepared to hold a beauty contest for Alex's sperm just yet. Instead, I headed to the personal products aisle of our local drugstore for an ovulation predictor kit. I marveled at the number of products available to detect hormone changes. Not surprisingly, ovulation kits were positioned right next to the pregnancy kits. The logic being: if this, then that. *Hardly.* As I stood comparing one brand with another I heard the fussing of a youngster coming from another aisle in the store. A double stroller pushed by a haggard-looking young woman who could not have been any older than twenty-two suddenly wheeled around the corner.

"Momma," yelled one of two restless toddlers trying to escape the stroller. The woman sighed heavily, quickly reached up for a pregnancy test and stuffed it in her purse. With fear in her eyes, she glanced up at me, silently pleading not to report her. She hurriedly turned the stroller around, wheeled it up the aisle and out of the store. I was momentarily stunned and stood for a minute holding the ovulation kit, astonished at the opposing circumstances that brought us to the drug store at the same moment in time – both anxious in our own way.

When I needed a mommy fix, I called my brother and sister-in-law, who were now expecting their second, to get time with my niece.

I watched with longing as they went about their mommy-and-daddy routine nestled in the heart of suburbia. While I entertained my niece with a game of "Candy Land," Alex comfortably stood sipping a beer on the other side of the screen door. He was wing man to my barbecuing brother, clad in a Hawaiian shirt, flipping hamburgers on the grill. It was a scene straight out of the '50s.

A Weber grill aficionado, Alex offered, "Did you know you can get Webers equipped with white wall tires?"

"Alex," my brother said with mock seriousness as he reached for his beer. "I have so much to learn from you."

My niece jumped up and slid the screen door open with a bang. "Uncle Alex, I won, I won."

"You're a true Mahoney girl," he said as he scooped her up effortlessly. "Always happiest when you come out on top. How 'bout a game of Simon Says?"

Alex's inner boy came out. With a twinkle in his eye and mock seriousness to spare he directed my niece into all sorts of silly poses. My giggling stopped when I heard my sister-in-law take a call from a friend who was getting ready for her first Lamaze class. A discussion I had overheard weeks earlier came back to me. I was uncomfortably and enviously surveying a room full of pregnant women as I awaited my annual gynecological exam. (Given the amount of time I was spending in doctor's offices I envisioned a new career as a waiting room critic. *You call these outdated magazines reading material? These seat cushions are hard as rocks. Would it kill you to have them restuffed?*) A sleep-deprived mother cradling a newborn while trying to keep a toddler under control was lecturing a newly pregnant woman sitting nearby, "You'll find when your baby arrives that it's no longer just about you anymore. Your children will provide the new mile markers in your life."

The conversation haunted me. Would I just be running in place without those mile markers to shape and define my life? While Alex and I considered the more advanced baby-making courses, we continued working hard on the basics. Alex noted ruefully that "this reproduction thing took all the fun out of sex." And he was right. Sex on demand dampened the flames of passion. The last thing we wanted to do was hop in the sack and get it on when it was mandatory. Sex goes from fun to work in no time when you feel like nothing more than a mating machine.

After almost another year of negative pregnancy test results and more head scratching from ob-gyns trying to piece the clues together, Alex and I reluctantly agreed we were ready to graduate to the next round of medical intervention. IUI, or intra-uterine insemination, is the junior varsity of "I" related treatments. An IUI is about as fun as it sounds. A doctor would insert the best looking of Alex's sperm – following a meticulous review of a sample provided earlier – into my uterus at the best possible time for fertilization. You have no idea how badly I wanted success so we wouldn't have to keep up this weird biological courtship or, worse, graduate to the grand-daddy of treatments: IVF. Initial research on the IVF process terrified me. There were so many drugs, screenings and tests, so many ways to screw up.

The IUI result: Negative.

On the eve of my thirty-sixth birthday in June I saw an advertisement in our morning newspaper containing a radiant woman holding an infant with the headline, "Having Trouble Conceiving?" YES! As a matter of fact I am. I placed a call and made an appointment to learn more.

I tried to distract myself with new work projects. I was in the copy room preparing materials for an early afternoon meeting when I heard someone behind me. It was Kim, an assistant in her early thirties, sporting a small but growing belly. In her hand she held the first ultrasound images of her three-month pregnancy.

"Hi, I hope I'm not bothering you," she said without waiting for an answer. She followed me back to my office. "I'm just back from the doctor with my new son's first pictures!"

"Ah." I said trying valiantly to muster some form of enthusiasm. "So you found out you're carrying a boy?"

"Yes. My two-year-old will have a little brother to play with – and to bully no doubt. My oldest is already the biggest boy in his daycare."

Kim prattled on but all I could focus on was the image of the little baby-like form in the ultrasound photo she had laid on my desk.

My mind reached back to the ultrasound image of my promising egg follicle just ahead of my IUI procedure two weeks earlier.

I suddenly stood up, interrupting Kim's monologue about what it would be like to have two boys. "It's a beautiful first photo," I said. "You and your husband are very fortunate."

Looking at my watch I added, "I'm sorry I have to be at a meeting." She didn't need to know it was still more than an hour from starting.

Kim moved into the hallway still talking, moving to the topic of the need to invest in some new maternity clothes as I reached into my drawer to grab my car keys and purse. As I rushed down the stairs to the lobby I began to hyperventilate. I pushed open the glass doors looking out over the parking lot trying to remember where I parked my car. Gulping air, I realized I had to calm down before I could even think about driving. Once behind the wheel, I turned on the air conditioning in the hopes that the cool air would counteract the burning tears forming in my eyes.

I needed a place to escape where mommies and babies were not likely to be. Seemed the harder I tried to get pregnant, the more pregnant women popped up around me reminding me that my stomach was way too flat. You know you've really got the pregnancy Jones bad when a flat stomach leaves you feeling less than feminine. It was the first time I actually craved a pooch, a bump. If I had been a little more like Oliver Stone, I might have hatched a conspiracy theory to explain all of the mommies-to-be – something way more exciting than that old "something in the water" explanation. Since no safe prego-free zone existed, I drove around a bit trying to calm down. I suddenly wondered what would become of my journals and photo albums if there were no children or grandchildren. They might never find curious offspring trying to piece together a set of lives that came before them. They wouldn't find their way into the family shrine common in most homes. In my parents' house the high school diploma of my paternal grandfather, Edward, was featured in the family room. Photos of Alex's parents and his father's patent awards hung in our makeshift home office. Each of the framed faces or accomplishments signified that although they were no longer alive, they had made an important contribution. Their legacy was those of us who were making our ways today.

It was our future son or daughter I had in mind as I held Alex's hand tightly in the widely advertised "fertility" clinic – no negatives – "infertility" would be bad marketing. We were there for an initial conversation with one of the lead physicians, one Dr. NoNonsense. Just before our audience with him I watched Alex flip the pages of a dog-eared magazine. I knew, based on the speed with which he was turning pages that he couldn't possibly be reading any of it. He had been the model of steadiness while I'd been caught up in our pregnancy quest. He could always find the bright side, like telling me he knew for a fact he was getting way more sex than any of his friends who'd recently became daddies. He put up with my moodiness and random outbursts of frustration with exceptional patience even after I practically ripped his head off for innocently suggesting we visit friends who had recently delivered their first child.

"What part of 'I can't be around new mommies' don't you understand?" I snapped at him. "Sure, you'll go watch sports and I'll be stuck getting chapter and verse about sleep deprivation and sore nipples. I don't think so!"

He got the last word in as he left for his weekly basketball game. "Pam, we can't go around the rest of our lives avoiding people with kids."

Now I could tell from his heavy sighs that he was the more uncomfortable of the two of us in the waiting room for a mid-day doctor appointment. He hated hospitals and doctors' offices. They brought back terrible memories of the sad and awful time he had spent in them with his father. He also knew that with each new round of physicians he had to once again submit to the humiliating act of providing sperm samples. The brown paper bag used to transport his precious cargo was no longer associated with lunch.

Once inside the doctor's office we faced a wall of diplomas from the Harvard Medical School and citations from the American Fertility Association. Alex and I both sat straight up in our chairs, prepared for yet another series of probing, awkward questions about our sex lives and respective medical histories. *Look, seriously, we know where to put it and when!*

The interrogation complete, the doctor pushed back his chair. "Let me be frank here. There's still a great deal we don't know about what interferes with conception and pregnancy. I'd want to pursue an aggressive therapy. We hold monthly IVF orientation sessions at the hospital auditorium next door. It's more efficient than trying to answer couple's questions one-on-one. The session also includes our finance manager who can discuss various payment plans. Most of our patients' insurance plans don't cover IVF procedures or the required drugs."

Alex's face flushed, signaling anger. He was clearly put off by the doctor's cavalier attitude. "I can appreciate that it's more *efficient* for you to defer questions to a group session, but it's hard for me to believe you know enough about either of us to determine that IVF is our next stop."

"I understand your frustration," Dr. NoNonsense countered. "I've treated hundreds of couples in similar predicaments. You have to trust that we're experienced enough to quickly assess the symptoms associated with infertility. If I could help you get pregnant tomorrow using IUI or other low-tech techniques that won't break the bank, I'd be happy to do so. I simply don't want to waste your time and raise false hopes of a successful outcome with a course of treatment that, frankly, I don't think will work for you."

I was taken aback by the doctor's candor and pessimism. It was the first time I'd encountered a physician convinced that our bodies were duds.

"If you're interested in signing up for the next IVF information session, it's next Tuesday evening," he said as he stood up. "It will provide you with the data you need to decide if you'd like to proceed."

With that we realized our audience with the good doctor was over. Based on my research into how fertility clinics operated, they were most interested in boosting the number of live births – if a few cycles didn't result in a baby it hurt their success standing. Successful stats were fertility clinics' primary marketing tool. Since they were not regulated, the clinics had discretion about which techniques they'd recommend. They also set their own age limits for couples they were willing take as patients. Since the vast majority of treatments weren't covered by insurance, couples relied on clinic data to determine which they wanted to use. Naturally they gravitated to clinics with the best stats. It was an odd catch-22.

That night Alex arrived home later than usual; we no longer commuted together. He headed investor relations at a tech company. Its business model boiled down to raising enormous amounts of capital to build under-utilized wireless data networks. Ironically, the CEO had previously run Enron and the CFO was destined to later work his magic at Pets.com. In retrospect, the Chapter 11 looming on the horizon couldn't have been more preordained. While Alex and a new CEO made the rounds delivering the bad news of a pending bankruptcy to stakeholders, his phrase "If you're going to get restructured just lay back and enjoy it" became the dominant thread of black humor. I could tell by way he dropped his briefcase and threw the mail on the counter that he wasn't in the mood to relive our latest sex life recital. It had been upsetting for me, too. I was still not ready to confront the subject of *in vitro* fertilization – at least not yet.

I stood in the kitchen chopping vegetables to make a stir fry. Caught up in the frustration of having to make such surreal decisions, I was growing increasingly agitated. My knife sliced into a broccoli with increasing violence. Alex took notice. "Whoa. Be careful with that knife. We don't need any John Bobbitt moments here, accidental or otherwise."

Alex had been on the receiving end of too many of my rants so I attributed my anger to a problem with an engineering team at work. He knew there was more at stake than disagreements with engineers, but he was clearly relieved when I left the explanation there. Neither of us had the energy to take the conversation back to the doctor's office. Instead we had an unspoken truce. Following dinner we tuned into a NOVA television segment on global warming which allowed us to escape from what would have otherwise been a difficult and prolonged discussion.

The closest we came to acknowledging what was really on our minds was when Alex observed, "Unlike *some* scientific matters at least there's consensus on what causes global warming."

Neither of us was feeling the least bit amorous when we turned in for the evening. I lay in bed unable to fall asleep. The irony of the situation was not lost on me. The increasing talk about malfunctioning sex organs contributed to a cooling off of our otherwise active, enjoyable sex life. Fortunately I was not ovulating so there was no added pressure to perform. Lying in the dark, the doctor's voice rang in my head, allowing night-time demons ample opportunity to torture me further.

Who are you kidding? You'll never conceive. You heard the pessimism in his voice. You've got a flawed womb. No amount of scientific intervention is going to fix your uterus.

Alex tossed and turned in the dark next to me. He clearly was having his own bout of insomnia. The last thing I wanted to do was to compound his misery by having him listen to me cry myself to sleep. As quietly as I could, I slipped out of bed and grabbed my latest non-scientific reading, a historical novel. I tiptoed slowly, struggling to make it out the doorway without the benefit of light. Just as I reached the threshold Alex called out in a soft voice, "What's wrong?"

"Oh, just preoccupied that's all," I said. "My mind is racing so I think it's best if I just try to settle my thoughts by reading a bit. I don't want to disturb you with the light. I'll sleep in the guest room."

When he didn't try to talk me out of it I continued into the room next door and attempted to pick up where I'd left off in my novel. Mercifully, it wasn't more than an hour before I fell asleep with the light on, the book's pages splayed open where I'd dropped off.

Infertility had become the elephant in the room. I'd read about infertility but never heard anyone actually acknowledge dealing with it. Apparently infertility didn't discriminate. It affected men and women of all races, colors and creeds equally. For eons it had struck families here there and everywhere – sisters and brothers, aunts and uncles, friends, colleagues and people crowding malls or strolling through parks.

What made me feel so alone was that, short of one woman who sadly cautioned some of the young pups in the office a few years earlier "not to wait" because time hadn't helped her, I didn't know anyone who had actually been diagnosed with any conditions remotely linked to infertil-ity. The conditions were well-disguised. I certainly didn't (and still don't) look infertile. Therein lay a big, big challenge.

Those of us trying to overcome or accept infertility were everywhere and yet nowhere. I started studying more closely people sitting next to me in restaurants, on planes, the sports stadium, the city council meeting room, the workplace or gym trying to pick out which ones didn't seem to have kids. It was next to impossible to know for certain who was fertile and who was not. We lacked readily identifiable symbols, matching uni-forms or trademark moves. I'd begun imagining what the reaction might be if I were brave enough to wear a t-shirt carrying the words "World's Best Infertile" much like parents who donned garb or bumper stickers reading "World's Best Dad." Couples without children in public places didn't offer definitive clues. They could either have left their little ones in the care of babysitters or made the decision not to have them. But if they were like me, they carried around a secret. They were humiliated at worst or distressed at best because they couldn't conceive. It's not surpris-ing then that infertility has been called the silent disorder. Very few, if any, people talk about it because it's too painful and let's face it, there is a shame associated with it. Who introduces themselves at neighborhood get-togethers, "Hey, the name's Bill and I'm sterile."

"Oh, you don't say! I'm Fredricka and I'm barren as the moon's sur-face. Great to meet you."

No, it's usually, "Hi, I'm Larry, father of those two strapping boys over there. You got any kids?"

"Well, Larry, I'm Katie and, yes, I've got three little ones. There they are – can you see the resemblance? They about drive me out of my mind most days. Fortunately this neighborhood has enough other kids to keep them busy."

Silent disorder indeed. The more I learned, the more it seemed in-fertility was the silent *plague*. I was part of the 7.3 million couples in the U.S. who had trouble conceiving. Let me put that number in perspective. Problems conceiving touch the number of people equivalent to all the citizens of Virginia or Israel or the residents of the nine-county San Francisco Bay area. And worldwide? The number is 50 to 80 million. To put *that* in some context, consider that Italy has just over 59 million citizens and Germany has 82 million.

While it may seem hard to imagine, Alex and I still managed to have something resembling a life outside of trying to conceive. I took a new position – this time a marketing role at a venture capital firm. While each of our job changes offered greater salary, benefits and perks, there was no coverage for fertility treatments.

One other significant life change took place around this time. Alex and I got married. He popped the question on the eve of the millennium. While I put the finishing touches on hors d'oeuvres for friends who would join us for a New Year's Eve celebration, Alex, dressed handsomely in a tux, poured us each a glass of Alexander Valley Cabernet Sauvignon. He popped a CD in the player and drew me into an impromptu dance.

While Eric Clapton sang to us, Alex pulled me close and looked earnestly into my eyes. "Pammie, what do you think of becoming my wife?"

Not sure if he was pulling my leg, I studied his face closely for a clue. He grew concerned at my lack of immediate response.

"Well, if you're asking me to marry you…" I responded tentatively.

"Yes," he said as if trying to convince himself as much as me. "Yes I am."

"Then," I said, pausing ever so slightly, "my answer is YES, of course, it's yes."

His face lit up and he held me in a tight embrace. Then he started to laugh and shake his head in disbelief. He had no ring to present. He hadn't actually planned on proposing. It was purely spontaneous. And, the spontaneity – so long absent from our lives, felt positively *magnificent*.

More importantly, our getting married felt absolutely right. I never doubted that we would spend the rest of our lives together, but becoming husband and wife was icing on the cake. The rest of the night I walked on air, swept up in the magic of the moment. There was no other man who lit up my world the way he did. He brought out the best in me. With him by my side I knew everything would always be okay.

We eloped to Hawaii. Alex told friends afterwards that it was time for me to make an honest man out of him. Our all-too-brief honeymoon started the minute we arrived on the island of Maui. No outrageous wedding tab or rehearsal dinners to fund. No guest lists to fret over, no worries about flowers, bands or tussles among the relatives. It was such a contrast to my first ceremony, with me hanging out in a crypt.

I found a wedding planner online in Hawaii who arranged for us to get access to a private beach fragrant with tropical flowers. She was one of our witnesses. A photographer was the other. We stood at the edge of a peninsula overlooking the Pacific while a statuesque, dignified yet barefoot native Hawaiian non-denominational minister in a church robe married us. As he completed the ceremony with a melodic Hawaiian blessing, a gentle tropical breeze caressed us and waves softly crashed far below. Among the many happy thoughts rushing through my mind: what a wonderful story this will be to share with our children.

Later that afternoon I watched Alex's muscular body emerge from the surf. The sun seemed to turn his Mediterranean skin instantly bronze. He stared down at me in my bikini approvingly. "I can't believe I've let a parade of doctors look at you naked. They should be paying me for the privilege."

The only other curiosity during our stay on the island was being "stalked" by Pierce Brosnan. We could not shake that guy to save our lives. Our first afternoon by the pool at a resort hotel he sat a few chairs away. As I casually reached for my Mai Tai, I turned to Alex and whispered, "I don't want to alarm you but it appears 007 is casing the joint." The next day when we went down to the spa for massages, there he was, robed in the waiting area, clearly anticipating our arrival. That night while Alex and I looked to catch some romantic time on the beach at sunset, 007 showed up with his squeeze. Then they followed us to dinner, and sat not far away in the dining room. Clearly 007 had to work on his unobtrusive shadowing skills. Alex came this close to telling him, "Look, we appreciate why you want to trace our every move but, really, we're on our honeymoon..."

Our honeymoon sex was amazing and frequent, but at the end of the month: NEGATIVE. Again.

CHAPTER THREE

BARGAINING: HOW MUCH TO BE LIKE EVERYONE ELSE?

The strange thing about reaching the end of a cycle was the impossibly wonderful ability to forget about what just *didn't* happen, replaced instead by the hope that the next month would, of course, be different. Yes, hope was a very powerful emotion, and there were clearly many in the fertility industry who wanted to sell hope when your own was lagging. I fell for their pitches every time. I was willing to bargain my way into pregnancy.

What have you got? Herbs? They don't look too scary. They're not outrageously priced. Sure, why not? My new hope came from an herbal formula sold in a bottle. According to a website that included a Stanford affiliation, these fertility-boosting herbs, conveniently in pill form, were to be taken three times a day by both the mother- and father-to-be. Alex looked at me with great skepticism when I told him the pills would make his sperm more robust and better formed. Bless him; he took them dutifully even though he thought I was becoming borderline psychotic. The herbs were a nice chaser to the "Yoga for Fertility" tape I'd found. There was a certain simpatico to herbs and yoga. Maybe I needed to start chanting, too?

Also on the list of new things to try: I learned that my health insurance covered visits to a chiropractor. I was a little scared about the possibility of getting my neck broken or my spine permanently injured, but

I was compelled to make the phone call when I read that adjustments to the spine can un-pinch mitigated nerve impulses, redirect their electrical energy to the uterus, and improve the odds of implantation, or something like that. Sign me up!

My first visit to the chiropractor's office left me more than a little doubtful. A young man no older than twenty-four, "the doctor," interviewed me to find out why I was seeking his help. I explained somewhat awkwardly that I'd not been able to conceive, that I was hoping he could direct his attention to making my womb more baby-friendly through spinal adjustments. The next thing I knew he closed his eyes and began praying over my womb!

I didn't know where to look as he summoned Jesus' help. Befuddled as he continued with his serious conversation with the Lord, I relented and decided that prayer of any kind certainly couldn't hurt. His impromptu soliloquy complete, he opened his eyes and instructed me to hop on the table. He positioned my neck and shoulders for my first spinal adjustment. The popping noise – and the spiritual encounter that had preceded it – was a tad disturbing, but not enough to keep me from scheduling a series of regular appointments.

I discovered and sampled various homeopathic remedies. After searching my local health food store I found a raspberry tea aimed at "soothing the uterus." The description on the box was promising enough:

> "Raspberry Leaf tea supports female systems. Its long history of safe human consumption is evident over thousands of years of use by women in Europe and North America to support healthy menstruation, strengthen and tone the uterus, and to prepare the womb for childbirth. Infusions of raspberry leaf have been traditionally used as an important gynecological aid by women of the Cherokee, Iroquois and Mohawk nations of North America. The British Herbal Pharmacopoeia indicates its use as a preparative for childbirth."

Bring it!

Okay. So, apparently compulsory relaxing, homeopathic tonics and the JV medical treatments weren't the answer. My womb needed some serious improvement. I got that message loud and clear. I had to let go of a long-held dream that went something like this:

One morning I would wake up feeling out of sorts. I would be a bit grumpier and more tired than normal. I'd have the appetite of a lumberjack. Suspicious, I would reach for a calendar and count back dates to figure out when "Aunt Flo" had last paid a visit. I would gulp down two big glasses of water and reach into the medicine cabinet for an at-home pregnancy test, a pee stick. I would clumsily follow the instructions on the box and wait impatiently for three minutes. Before my very eyes two unmistakable bright pink lines would emerge. Elated, I would eagerly plan how I would share the happy, unexpected news with Alex.

I might greet him with a stork-shaped helium-filled Mylar balloon. If he was like most guys, he would miss the symbolism; perhaps mistake the stork for a flamingo and assume I was lobbying for a trip to the tropics. I would slug him playfully in the arm and speak the words that have rocked the sensibility of men throughout civilization.

"You're going to be a daddy."

His expression would change from confusion to sheer joy. He would scoop me up in his arms and we would eagerly start to plan for our baby. Two years later we would have another child, and then not long after that a third before deciding, what with so many play dates and competing soccer schedules, not to mention skyrocketing college tuition fees, our family was complete...

Daydreams aside, in real life our next big trip took us in December to Ireland. In a damp, dimly lit church the baptismal font was slightly obscured behind stone columns but I could see Alex clearly. His neatly trimmed beard and balding head gave him the look of Sean Connery. He stood in the church alcove as straight and tall as if he were awaiting inspection in the Navy, with his hand on the shoulder of our four-year-old nephew, also named Alex after his uncle. His parents had delayed the baptism a few years and combined this ceremony with our Christmas visit to Dublin where they lived. We were not in a Catholic church but the Church of Ireland, in part because Ungle Alex (as our nephew called him) and his brother had been confirmed in an Episcopalian church. Our nephew was in line to attend a school associated with this particular church and it helped to be part of the congregation. Before the ceremony began I took the opportunity to pray for you-know-what. I may have been severely jetlagged but it occurred to me that the Church of Ireland God might not be as busy as the Catholic God. *Um, Excuse me. Yes, over here in bench two, third column over. I'm new here but look, I've been through the more rigorous, guilt-inducing religious training at the church down the street. Any chance you're willing to hear a request for a pregnancy?*

I'm not going to lie. It stung more than a little to watch Alex stand up in the role of godfather while I was relegated to simply the wife of the godfather. This was the second time I'd been passed over and sat through a baptism for a nephew or niece without being directly involved. Seems I couldn't score as a mother or a godmother. Not that I was a paragon of spiritual life but I was hardly a complete derelict either. *Sigh.* My self-esteem took another hit. The message was clear: *Not qualified. Apply again when you've proven you've got the right stuff.* Once more I felt like a failure.

While I was distracted by R&D efforts in fertility land, Silicon Valley started to implode. Almost overnight it came to resemble a battleground, dead and dying companies strewn everywhere. Block after block of empty office buildings. Unemployment skyrocketed. People loaded up U-Haul trucks and headed out of town. The reverse migration left the once bustling and optimistic area with an eerie calm and sense of doom. It was hardly the time to be focused on family creation but that didn't stop Mother Nature from fighting back and refilling the ranks her own way. Three new pregnancy announcements were made rapid-fire-like in my office: bam, bam, BAM!

Trapped in a conference room there was no escape. I swallowed hard, trying to control the ugly green monster, and steeled myself for the baby talk and swelling bellies that were going to be with me for the next six months. Meanwhile on the home front, I couldn't seem to find an escape either. Not long after Alex returned from a business trip, friends made a jubilant declaration that they were pregnant with their second. The four of us had been out to dinner at a popular restaurant on an unseasonably warm night. When the waiter brought over the wine list our daddy friend made a show of hiding it from his wife and told her that, despite the heart-friendly characteristics of red wine and her love of Cabernet, he had to look out for the health and well-being of their baby-to-be. "No wine for the mommy."

As the news settled in I felt the blood drain from my face. Alex got up and walked over to hug our beaming pregnant friend and slug his pal's arm playfully. My better half was a born diplomat and, unlike me, was able to separate out his own stuff from someone else's, enabling him share in the joy of others. I wished I'd been granted the same capacity. I drank more than my share of Cabernet to try to forget that I wasn't in the family way. My period had arrived that morning.

The next morning as I fought a hangover Alex gently reminded me that a baby conceived or born to someone else doesn't mean there are fewer babies available to us. Despite the soundness of his logic it didn't make me feel any better. With each passing month I felt worse, under siege. Once benign, everyday occurrences like baby showers became barbaric in a special sort of way and, not surprisingly, there were lots of them. I was now at an age where baby showers were as regular as summer thunderstorms in Michigan. If I were putting the infertility experience on the stage through an avant-garde lens I would have cast my mood as the black clouds, my uterus as the petulant protagonist, and women who planned baby showers as Lucifer's chorus girls. Ah, there was so much more to do there with the stagecraft but I had to get my game face on for the real life baby-palooza awaiting me.

One shower in particular challenged me like no other. A cute invitation had arrived a few weeks earlier. What made that one worse than the rest was that the guest of honor was one of the women I had always assumed would be my pregnancy pal, the woman who had once cavorted with me on the deck of the Star Princess. She had divorced and remarried, too. Our babies were supposed to roll around together on a blanket, toddle together and grow up to be great friends like us. She was off to the races and I was still stuck in the barn. The slings and arrows came at me as I walked into the living room. Around a centerpiece of a stork carrying its bundle for delivery stood a group of women. They were comparing notes and one-upping each other about their last pregnancies.

"I was sick from day one! And I'm not just talking morning sickness. My doctor kept telling me that it would be over at the end of the first trimester. Well it wasn't! I'd call it 24/7 sickness."

"The skin on my abdomen has never fully recovered. A two-piece bathing suit? That ain't ever gonna happen again!"

"My breasts got so large I had to get a custom-designed bra. I had no choice. The straps on those off-the-shelf maternity bras cut a permanent groove into my shoulders. Rich called them my 'Pamela Anderson breasts,' but I wouldn't let him get anywhere close. They might be fun for him, but sex was the last thing on my mind."

I smiled wanly and moved to the kitchen. There on the floor was an empty dog cage. It belonged to an adorable puppy out for a walk with the man of the house. My friend and her husband didn't want their child-to-be to grow up without a pet. Until he could pass obedience school, the furry little mutt had to spend most of his time behind bars. In my own way I could relate to his prisoner status. At that very moment I was feeling like I had no escape myself.

Once all the guests arrived and settled in, the games began. Each woman received a white onesie. An enthusiastic craft lover instructed us to move about the house to sample different paint colors and gather inspiration for a custom-decorated result. There would be a vote later for the most creative. I was not feeling particularly inspired and simply wanted to get through the exercise. I reached for the blue and yellow paint and set to work on mastering a University of Michigan "M" and underneath write "Future Wolverine."

The afternoon moved agonizingly slowly and was made all the more excruciating when each woman was instructed to write down on a slip of paper either a favorite motherhood memory or motherhood advice. All of the memories and advice were deposited through a slot in a colorfully decorated Pampers box. My friend's job was to pull out one of the notes and read it aloud, trying all the while to guess its author. What followed was a mesh of treasured and personal recollections and experiences that all but broke my heart. There were pregnancy and birth-related memories, some with little hints associated with them:

"I knew I was a mother the first time I felt my baby kick – and he clearly inherited the size of his feet from my side of the family."

Each memory read aloud prompted a laugh or a knowing nod of agreement.

Looking around the room, I realized that I was the only one who had not crossed into the realm of motherhood. The advice I penned was motivated not by experience but by what I had heard every other parent echo as their children grew up too fast.

"Cherish every adoring gaze and all the spontaneous hugs and kisses you get while your kids are still young enough not to be embarrassed or curbed by independence."

After two wrong guesses at the author a light bulb went on in my friend's head. "Pam. It's Pam who wrote this."

I nodded while the woman seated next to me said, "But I didn't think you had any kids."

I cringed while the rest of the room broke out in a chorus of related unwanted suggestions.

"Now, don't you worry. If you'd just relax more you'd get pregnant in a heartbeat."

"Have you tried those ovulation thingie kits? They worked for my sister-in-law."

"No. You don't need those! Just take a vacation. That's when it always happens."

"My friend got pregnant right after she adopted. I've heard that's pretty common."

"Take it from me, when you least it expect it, it will happen. Stop trying so hard."

"It will be your turn before you know it!"

That evening I was spent. My face muscles ached from being held in a perpetual false smile. My strength and energy had been eroded. The joyous laughter surrounding me all afternoon built to a crescendo, sapping my spirit a little more each time I had to feign interest in the best diaper strategy, the best feeding and burping regimen or the best sleeping strategy. I lay on the couch under a worn fleece blanket and stared into space unable to get up or move. The remote for the TV sat next to me but reaching for it and pushing the button took more effort than I could expend. My soul was bleeding.

That night memories of my Grandma Stella came back to me. What fascinated me most was her sunny outlook in the face of a stormy life. Among other things she suffered from arthritis. While I didn't know exactly what that felt like, I remembered how debilitating arthritis pain could be for her. At the same time, Grandma Stella loved to dance. There was always a radio in her kitchen tuned to a Polish station that played polkas. With smells of boiled cabbage filling the room, my siblings and I would watch and sometimes snicker when she hummed, a bit off tune, along with the melodies. She would dance at the sink and stove at times like a woman possessed. She seemed transported to another place and time. Now I looked back on her joyful outbursts with a new appreciation.

I realized that arthritis was a great metaphor for infertility. Sometimes it was a dull sensation, barely recognizable in the course of a day, but it was always there. Other times, like Grandma Stella, I ached too much to dance. It was becoming clear to me that each day brought a different degree of discomfort. Of course, I much preferred the days when I could dance and sing and feel good, but the pain always managed to find me again, delivering sharp pangs. On those days I was reminded how much effort it took for Grandma Stella to dance.

And it was indeed time to sign up for a new dance class. Among the routines would be a worrisome, difficult set of instructions involving powerful hormones, among other things. A few weeks earlier, inching along in rush hour traffic after a day fraught with office politics, I tried to imagine my life ten years forward: forty-seven and childless. I all but had a panic attack. Would I hate myself for not having at least *tried* IVF? While the idea of the procedure unnerved me, I was suddenly more afraid of the alternative. The theme from *Mission: Impossible* played in my head as I walked into the kitchen to start dinner.

The growl from the garage door opener signaled that Alex was home. I was defrosting leftovers in the microwave when he found me and gave me a kiss.

"How was your day?"

"Well … I've been thinking."

"Uh, oh, Pammie thinking. I'm not sure I like the sound of that."

I pulled down two plates from the cupboard. "Yeah, well, I'm thinking it might be time to push further ahead on the reproductive front."

The microwave bell rang, piercing the silence. Alex carried the plates to the table without saying anything.

I took my seat. "So, what are your thoughts?"

"You know I want kids – a pack of them is what I always had in mind…" he began.

I tensed up as I waited for what would come next.

"It's just," he added slowly, "we're talking about a major medical procedure that even in the best of circumstances has a low success rate."

I sighed loudly.

"I did a little research," he added tentatively. "I found stats not biased by those profiting from infertility. There's this website from a U.K. agency that regulates IVF. It said only twenty-two percent of treatment cycles for women under thirty-eight actually result in a live birth. That's one in five."

I was not going to be dissuaded by statistics. "But what about those one in five who now have a baby?"

"It's about more than just the stats, Pam. I worry about the side effects of the drugs and, well, the potential for greater disappointment if it doesn't work."

I paced the room while my dinner grew cold.

"I've heard directly from guys who have been through it."

Apparently more than basketball took place in the gym. They had actual conversations.

"What they describe isn't pretty," he continued. "The drug regimen is brutal – not for them, for their wives. Two or more hormone injections a day into the abdomen or thighs – with swelling and bruising. And the mood swings they described make Dr. Jekyll and Mr. Hyde seem normal. Why any husband would willingly inject his wife with more hormones is beyond me…

"The worst part, though," he said quietly, "was hearing from one of the guys who followed all the steps exactly as instructed. The result was the same: no pregnancy – and that's after four and five rounds with IVF. His company took IVF coverage off of their medical insurance plan because of him. It just doesn't seem to make any sense…"

I could wait no longer, and interrupted. "None of it makes any sense! Does it make sense that we're a healthy, well-educated, hard-working couple who can't make a baby? Does it make sense that men and women who wouldn't know a healthy meal if it was sitting in front of them, do drugs, can't or won't take care of themselves, let alone find a stable relationship, still manage to crank out kids?

"Does it make sense that there are lousy parents out there who weren't really sure they wanted kids in the first place but had them anyway? Does it make sense that healthcare insurance will pay for diabetes treatment for people who practically eat themselves to death but won't cover any attempts to fix a broken uterus or slow-swimming sperm?"

That's when Alex jumped back in. "I don't want money to be the sole factor in deciding whether we move ahead, but we also need to be rational here. From what the guys tell me, the average cost of an IVF cycle is anywhere from $13,000 to $17,000 – all of it out of pocket.

"You see the bills. You know with our mortgage, hell, with any mortgage in Silicon Valley, we haven't exactly been socking away money," he added. "What would happen if we had an emergency?"

I realized Alex was right, but the desire to get pregnant with his baby was so strong that any rational argument was beyond my comprehension at that moment. Seeing tears well up in my eyes he immediately got up to embrace me. I slumped in his arms and the tears began to fall.

"But I want so much to have *our* child," I said quietly. "I want it so badly it hurts. It's all I can think about."

"I know. I know how much it means to you," he said stroking my hair, adding softly. "A little Pammie, that's something I want very much, too."

The sound of rain slapping against the windows suddenly filled the room. Alex held me until my breathing quieted and the tears stopped. Neither one of us had an appetite anymore.

"Okay, then," Alex said with some reservation. "If you're ready to go for the shots, and all the unpleasant stuff that comes with IVF, I'll look over all of our expenses and work up a budget for IVF."

I was grateful beyond words. I needed to feel as though we were still in control, that we weren't simply going to stand by idly when there were options at our disposal.

While no longer a practicing Catholic, I knew the Church frowned upon tampering with the reproductive organs either in the prevention or making of new life. With the decision made to proceed, try as hard as I could *not* to let guilt play too large a role in my life, it dogged me. I was raised Catholic, after all. My not-so-great standing with the church only added to my stress level and worrying. They had an opinion on everything and it usually ran counter to mine. So why, after divorce and living in sin, did the rigid church doctrine matter? Beats the hell out me. It made no sense at all. Rationally I wanted to believe that we would be using the tools and learning that were made possible by God's very creations, but still something about the Vatican's disapproval made me feel bad. Not bad enough, though, *not* to try what was available. I felt seriously wicked nonetheless and didn't tell my parents what we were planning.

My new home away from home that spring between business trips and project deadlines became a research hospital. Inside it was the Reproductive Endocrinology and Infertility clinic – the "REI" for those of us who know it best. It sits on a world-famous campus in Silicon Valley that starts with an "S". To find the REI you have to go to the third floor of the hospital and take a right. If you walk too far you'll end up in the Neurology Clinic. Trust me, after the endless series of tests and probing of my private bits, I thought more than once about going there to have my head examined.

The REI waiting room resembled a mini United Nations. From the looks of the place there was no prototypical "infertile couple." While there were a few sheepish expressions (mine included), the vast majority seemed resigned to being in this dog-eared but bustling clinic. Clearly by the time you're hanging out in a research hospital you'd moved beyond the acute shock and embarrassment that accompanies the first infertility diagnosis. I watched one young, hip woman wave at another as she entered the clinic. The two huddled together talking quietly. I could make out part of their dialogue. I was both fascinated and a bit repulsed.

"I'm really happy with the acupuncture you recommended," said one in a barely concealed whisper. "My egg follicles are *much* more developed than last month at this time."

"Cool," the other responded. "Doesn't the acupuncture totally relax your mind? Beats the hell out of the usual IVF mental torture. During my sessions I just let go and let the needles do their work."

A team of nurses kept things moving. One by one they called out the names of female patients and ushered them to one of a series of small examining rooms. There the female patient waited to be prodded and assessed all the while wrapped in a paper gown that made loud crumpling noises when adjusted. The male patients either waited with their partners or were sent one by one – there was lots of coming and going – to a small institutional room with dull, white tile walls. I got the lowdown on the "guy" room from Alex. Behind a door sporting a picture of a baby's face and these words written underneath –"the future is your hands" – was a former restroom with the usual toilet stall, urinal and sink. Mounted high in one corner, much like a sports bar, was a television set and VCR. The second addition to the room was a small cabinet with a countertop where the remote control for the TV and VCR sat. Across the face of the bottom drawer of the cabinet was a strip of white hospital tape on which the word "videos" was written with a black marker. The top drawer had a similar makeshift label with the word "magazines." Each magazine, from soft to hard core porn, had "Property of Stanford Hospital – do NOT remove" scribbled in magic market across the cover. (There, I've given it away. Stanford did more than spawn startups; it also treated people trying to spawn.) Alex wondered how they justified the porn purchases to the university accounting department.

Masturbation on command with your choice of smut. And if that wasn't bad enough, an army of white coats lay in wait just outside the door to screen the results of your orgasm. Was this really the best medical science had to offer?

On my first visit to the REI I went solo. No razzle-dazzle just yet. I was there to get my fluids checked, get my tires kicked, so to speak. This consultation came after what had felt like an endless losing season of do-it-yourself-attempts to get pregnant. We excelled at fielding and at-bats but we couldn't manage a win. Each cycle started the same way and included a series of positive ovulation pee sticks (I ovulate like a champ, by the way), followed two weeks later by a BFN – infertility lingo for Big Fat (or F*&ing) Negative – on a never-ending sequence of evil single-line pregnancy tests that seemed intent on mocking me.

Waiting my turn in the hospital examining room, worries raged: How much longer will this take? And why is it so difficult? All around the globe for centuries on end couples naturally conceived and delivered children, raised them and then became grandparents. Lather, rinse and repeat. But what would it mean to never have such rites of passage? Would I ever fully become a woman if I never experienced the full life cycle? Those questions never came up in any rap sessions I'd overheard. My women's studies class at UofM hadn't offered up any clues.

At Stanford we learned there were more than a few risks involved with aggressive infertility treatments. One study revealed that women taking hormones and other super-charged fertility drugs to stimulate greater egg production were at risk from life-threatening side effects. This sentence from a scientific article would be a show stopper for many:

"They say that the powerful drugs given to the volunteers to help increase the number of eggs they produce can cause paralysis, limb amputation and even death."

But how do you talk sense to a woman, a 21st century woman no less – remember I can still be an astronaut if I want! – driven by the primal urge to reproduce? Did *real* women rely on hormones and ovulations kits to conceive? Would using these aids disqualify me from being a natural woman? Would the International Olympic Committee give me the heave-ho?

When it came time to purchase our IVF medications – nearly a dozen different injectables, pills, and suppositories – Alex created a spreadsheet to track the various drug combinations and administration times over a 30-day period. He made a second schedule that mapped out the multiple trips to the hospital for ultrasounds and other routine monitoring during the IVF cycle.

Proud of his work, he shared the results with me one Sunday morning during the halftime of a Detroit Pistons game. I was in the living room curled up on the sofa. It had been six years since I first went to the library to locate books about getting pregnant. Here I was, newly turned thirty-eight, earnestly reading the more advanced material: "*The Couple's Guide to In Vitro Fertilization,*" one of three books I checked out a few days earlier. The others in my reading stack: "*The Wayward Stork*" and "*When Nature's Not Enough.*"

"I see you've got a little light reading lined up for today," he observed before presenting his schedules with a flourish. "Whaddya think? I've drawn up a few plays here. You can call me Coach."

"Well, look at you!"

"Since this is will be my kid, too, it seemed only right that I get, well, involved," he added.

The pharmacy that supplied the medications was Disco Rex, which Alex observed would be a great name for a dinosaur disco. It was located just a few miles from the REI clinic and had a corner on the market for fertility drugs in the area. At a cramped counter space, a serious gray-haired man in a white coat carefully walked Alex through the nearly dozen prescriptions and explained how they were to be administered. To make sure he didn't forget any instructions, Alex took careful notes. With the tutorial complete the cashier, who had been off to the side listening intently, stepped forward to ring up his purchase. Apparently she had only started at the pharmacy a few days earlier and was amazed at what lay before her: paraphernalia only an addict (or an IVF patient) could fully appreciate. Piled on the counter were some seventy syringes, alcohol wipes, ampules, an industrial-sized container for used needles, and a large volume of assorted hormone medications, with scary names like recombinant FSH and gonadotropins, in liquid and pill form. There was even baby aspirin (yes, those little pills were also part of my regimen).

The cashier rang up the total and gasped. "Four thousand four hundred eighty dollars!? Do you have an insurance card?" Before Alex had a chance to respond, the pharmacist looked up from his work behind her and said, "This medication is rarely covered by insurance. It's typically an out-of-pocket expense for our customers."

The young woman turned back to face Alex and laughed nervously. "I'm sorry. I'm just amazed that you can do this. Forty-five hundred dollars for a pile of drugs! You must really want this baby."

Handing over his credit card and not quite sure how to respond, Alex signed his name on the receipt and mumbled, "Well, I do get frequent flier miles."

One morning a couple of days later as I made my way into the kitchen for my first cup of raspberry tea, I discovered Alex with a syringe in one hand, while the other pinched his flesh. I stopped so as not to break his concentration and watched as he inserted a needle into his lower belly. I waited until the needle was safely withdrawn before speaking.

"I hope you didn't use any of my hormones. Forget about what they might actually do to you. Those things are expensive!"

With a look of satisfaction Alex held up the needle and released the pinched flesh. "Nope, it is sterile water. I just had to know what you'd experience later this week when we start the meds. Now I understand what the injections feel like."

Curious, I asked, "And? What's the verdict?"

"A slight sting as the needle goes in," he told me, "but not seriously painful. The strangest part is how tough the outer skin layer is. I had to give it a pretty good jab. I guess I'm not as thin-skinned as I once thought!"

A few days later it was my turn. Alex had the syringe out and was preparing the hormone concoction when I arrived in the kitchen. The coffee maker gurgled and sighed as I pulled my sweater up to offer an area on my abdomen for the alcohol wipe. As I always did whenever I saw a needle, I looked the other way. Alex gamely inserted the shot just below and to the left of my belly button. I felt a burning sensation under my skin as he gently but quickly depressed the plunger to dispense the contents. He reached over to give me a kiss.

"Was it good for you?" he asked with a sympathetic smile.

I took the needle from him and discarded it in the red syringe disposal container provided by the hospital. "Yes, pass the cigarettes, please."

It had become a running gag. The shots were the closest thing to sex that we would have for several weeks outside of some couch-cuddling. Ironically, the doctors discouraged couples from engaging in conjugal visits – which only made us want sex more – while trying to make a baby through IVF. Go figure.

Some two weeks later I was on verge of my egg harvest. What strange imagery that term evoked, and not the warm and fuzzy kind. The mystery of what was really happening inside me would be revealed in a series of ultrasounds on a big screen in an examining room. This long-awaited reveal would not involve red carpets, paparazzi or popcorn. For each visit I had to fill my bladder to capacity and sit patiently, my legs tightly crossed, in the waiting room with the usual assortment of newbies and veteran patients filling well-worn chairs.

You'd be amazed at how matter-of-fact getting naked in front of strangers (assorted medical staff and technicians, not patients) had become – so much so that I resisted the urge to disrobe when I showed up for my six-month dental check up. I was getting positively German about my nakedness. I would have fit right in with the nude crowd at the Englischer Garden in Munich. My, my how things had changed since I had woken up from a nap during a college backpack trip amazed and aghast at being surrounding by Germans *au naturel* playing Frisbee and walking their dogs.

Once in the examining room the doctor squirted clear gel onto my abdomen. Then it was time for the "dildo cam," as I'd playfully overhead it called by the vets in the waiting room. On a monitor I watched with amazement as my ovaries came into view – first the left, then the right. With each visit, Dr. Marvelous (so nicknamed for his model bedside manner) used a computer keyboard and mouse to mark the coordinates and measure the size of my growing egg follicles. I studied his face closely looking for any clues that might signal his level of satisfaction. He calmly called out to the attendant numbers that sounded like a quarterback calling a play on the field:

"Right, 16, 13.5, 10, 9.5. Left, 16, 14.5, 13, 11.5, 9.5, 9.5."

I resisted the urge to shout out: "Hike!"

The numbers meant nothing to me until Dr. Marvelous explained that they were measurements, in millimeters, of the size of the egg follicles developing inside my left and right ovaries.

In my bathroom at home, with various pill containers fighting for counter space with moisturizers and makeup, I re-read the instructions provided by the hospital and prepared for bed. I lay down and realized that the swelling in my abdomen from my dozen or so growing egg follicles prevented me from comfortably sleeping on my stomach. I carefully turned onto my side, a smile creeping across my face.

This must be what it feels like to be pregnant, I thought triumphantly. A series of questions came next. *How soon will there be morning sickness? What will the first baby kick feel like? I wonder if there's a secret handshake for pregnant women.* Whenever I saw them together they all looked happily content in their mommy-to-be club comparing notes and belly sizes. It seemed it would only be a matter of time before my "newcomer's kit" arrived. It was the first bit of pure joy I allowed myself to feel since we started the demanding IVF protocol. We were with one of the best medical teams on the planet. For once the demon thoughts were drowned out by a more hopeful chorus. *Finally*, we've got this figured out. I reveled in the joyful expectation. It was the closest I had ever come to being pregnant.

On the morning of the egg retrieval my feet were ice cold even though I was wearing socks. I had been advised by the nurse to bring something to keep my feet warm. Apparently fasting caused the body to divert blood from the extremities to the more important organs. The nurse wasn't kidding. In a faded hospital gown I shook involuntarily under a thin blanket. Despite fourteen hours of fasting and the extreme hormones Alex had been injecting into me a few times a day, I felt surprisingly good, although a bit dehydrated. A different kind of clock, more like a stopwatch, was now ticking loudly in my head. I had less than an hour available to undergo a delicately timed surgical procedure – so delicate that if it didn't happen within a tightly prescribed window it would be a bust. The anesthesiologist was nowhere to be found. A serious problem to be sure. We couldn't start without him.

Alex had already completed his part of the exercise. Although the key to the masturbation room itself was no larger than a normal house key, it was attached to a half-inch thick block of wood about one-foot in length, emblazoned with the letters R.E.I. "Have problems with theft?" Alex asked the receptionist as he unsuccessfully tried to palm the key.

A nurse's assistant dropped a brown bag on the counter and ignored his halfhearted attempt at humor. The bag contained a sterile collection cup and two identification labels with instructions to affix one label to the side of the cup for identification and use the second to form a seal over its top. "You do know the location of the room and procedure?"

"Yes, I know the drill. Unfortunately, I'm a veteran of several campaigns," Alex replied to her blank face and stare.

He turned from the counter to begin what he had come to think of as "the walk of shame." To reach his destination he had to traipse through the fertility clinic's waiting room, past its fidgeting patients, then down the long hallway that led to the clinic. The absurd keychain, much too large to discreetly place in his pocket, made a very public announcement of his mission. The women he encountered along the way saw his cargo and quickly looked the other way. The men, on the other hand, gave him a sympathetic look.

Once Alex reached the busy main corridor, he turned to his left and walked a few steps before reaching the door of the converted restroom. Adding insult to injury, he told me later, the key resisted. Grossly underestimating his nervousness, he found it difficult to hold the lunch bag and cup in his left hand while trying to work a key weighed down by a small anchor in his right.

"Oh, damn!" he yelled as he dropped the key and its dramatically oversized keychain. The wood block landed with a loud thud, then energetically bounced over the floor, while the key merrily clinked along before finally settling in the middle of the corridor.

A male orderly, who just happened to be passing by pushing an empty wheelchair reached down, picked up the block of wood, and nonchalantly handed it over. "Need any help with that?"

"No, I'm sure I'll manage," Alex mumbled.

Efforts to regain his composure were soon rewarded as he finally worked the key into the lock and turned its reluctant tumblers. He slipped inside the room, pulled the door shut behind him, secured the latch and loudly exhaled. Alex later said he wasn't sure if he was more relieved to lock himself in or to lock the rest of the world out.

At 9 a.m. our anesthesiologist finally arrived. I was fully ready to proceed with the next step in pre-op when he informed us, apologetically, that he was being called into emergency surgery and would not be able to assist us. Another anesthesiologist would have to be called in from home.

It was the Fourth of July holiday weekend and the staff was thin. The unexpected wait intensified what had already been a nerve-racking pre-op. It had begun in earnest eleven hours earlier in our kitchen. That's when Alex had administered a particularly painful shot into my now black and blue speckled abdomen. The syringe contained a special kind of hormone. This was the big kahuna that, in turn, was to trigger my dozen egg follicles to ovulate.

At 9:30 one of the nurses volunteered to start my IV so we could make good use of the time available. The nurse looked at both of my arms and, with little confidence, informed me that I had very small, hard-to-find veins. Already on edge, I grew hyper-agitated. The nurse proceeded with what became a frustrating series of attempts to find a willing vein. Adrenaline and synthetic hormones coursed through my body. Tremendous anxiety reigned. As hard as I tried I simply could not stop shaking.

Like an animal sensing danger all of my senses were heightened. The hospital's antiseptic smell was overpowering, such a contrast to the flowering gloxinia that perfumed the air as we had left the house that morning. The sun had just come up over the foothills of the Santa Cruz Mountains as I climbed ever so gently into the passenger seat of Big Shirl. On the twenty-three-mile drive to Stanford Hospital, I snapped at Alex for driving over anything resembling a bump in the road. In my mind's eye they were the equivalent of land mines. If the off-road suspension on our Jeep encountered rough pavement, I was certain the vibrations would rattle or explode my fragile egg follicles. My guy, meanwhile, was worried about getting my follicles there on time.

I had tried to distract myself thinking about the previous two weeks of rigorously prescribed medications – replaying the schedule. Rather than counting sheep I was counting pills. Some went down the hatch only in the morning, others only at night. Then there were the shots. We alternated between my thighs and abdomen morning and night to allow the unavoidable bruises to heal. The last injection was precisely timed so that Dr. Marvelous could delicately retrieve my fragile eggs and hand them off to another set of experts in the lab who would have Alex's washed, screened and waiting sperm ready to inject into my eggs – all of us on my hardworking baby-making team hoping for fertilization. Fertilization, though, was only one in a series of stops on the bumpy road to pregnancy.

It was obvious that my agitation was interfering with the nurse's ability to locate a willing vein. Her attempts at humor – "It looks like you left your veins at home today" – didn't work to settle me down. In fact, they had the opposite effect. Finally, the nurse agreed to wait until the back-up anesthesiologist arrived. By this time, tears were streaming down my cheeks. Any of my attempts to stay cool, calm and collected had completely failed. I swallowed a sob.

I felt like a two-time loser. First, I needed to rely on a team of experts to get my eggs out for supervised fertilization, and now my bashful veins threatened to sabotage the needed retrieval. At the same time I was angry. We had done everything by the book throughout the weeks of pre-harvest treatment. I had been an obedient patient. During my checkups I accommodated, without complaint, other patients whose retrievals and transfers kept me waiting for up to one and a half hours past scheduled appointment times. We arrived early, as requested, for pre-op, and adding insult to injury we pre-paid $10,000 for all of the remaining lab and medical work required over the next two weeks. The holiday weekend appointment time left the hospital with reduced staff. I understood that. Emergency surgeries took precedence. I understood that, too. But I was about to ovulate and there was nothing I could do to stop it.

And then, finally, relief.

At 9:50 an anesthesiology resident and the doctor she was training under arrived. They clearly had been informed they would be encountering a patient who was pretty worked up because they got right down to business without any small talk. After fiddling with my IV and the needle they located a vein on the back of my left hand. After what seemed like an eternity, the time had come for me to go across the hall for the retrieval, escorted by a nurse wheeling my IV. Four people descended upon me in the operating room. I glimpsed Dr. Marvelous outside the door. Before I knew it, the anesthesia took effect. Just forty minutes later I awakened back in the room where I started. I quickly regained consciousness. Together with Alex we learned that the doctor had successfully retrieved ten eggs from ten follicles.

"One hundred percent is pretty unusual for someone with your ovarian reserve," an REI nurse informed us. The best of Alex's sperm sample were washed and ready. That news turned our worried expressions to relief. We smiled at each other and clucked contentedly like students who had just learned that we were well above average. Did we get a trophy of some kind?

After the euphoria in post-op wore off I lay weak and disoriented while around me the hospital buzzed with activity. I might have thought I was pretty special but no one was throwing me any parades or baby showers just yet. I almost passed out the first time I tried walking down the hall to the restroom. This was becoming a bad habit whenever I had surgery. Clearly anesthesia and I were not well suited to each other. A nurse rushed to get me into a wheel chair. Alex wheeled me into a vacant examining room with a sink. It was a good thing the sink was at the perfect height for a wheelchair-bound patient because I immediately lost the graham crackers and ginger ale they provided me a few minutes earlier to end my fast.

Alex rushed to get help. A nurse took my blood pressure. It was quite low. The lack of fluids and the pummeling my body had been through had caught up with me. I needed to lie down until I was strong enough to walk. That's when the pain in my abdomen kicked in. The human body, I recalled from my earlier surgery, didn't like it when internal organs were manipulated.

Alex noticed a small CD player in the room along with a few CDs that contained instrumental, classical or equally mellow selections.

"Hey, there's some music here," he said softly. "Would you like to hear something or would you prefer to just lie here quietly?"

"Music, honey," I said weakly. "Anything to take my mind off of this pain."

He grabbed the CD on top. Seconds later the soothing voice of Celine Dion singing "A New Day Has Come" filled the room. The song came out after Celine's successful delivery of her son. Her IVF had led to success so I tried to maintain a positive outlook. As the lyrics continued, Alex squeezed my hand a few times. With my other hand I gently rubbed my swollen, sore abdomen. I closed my eyes and listened as the words washed over me.

...A new day, oh..oh..
I was waiting for so long
For a miracle to come
Everyone told me to be strong...

Strength slowly returned to my body. Alex nervously paced and found a copy of the daily newspaper lying behind a chair. He looked for anything he could read aloud to distract me. He turned to the horoscopes and scanned down to the Gemini entry.

"Hey," he said his voice brightening. "Listen to this: Gemini. Despite the odds, you win the game. Cycle high; you will be at the right place at a critical moment almost effortlessly. Events will transpire to bring you closer to the ultimate goal."

I laughed somewhat painfully. Alex thought horoscopes were silly, but I appreciated his effort, nonetheless, to try to focus on the positive. The lightness in my head was gone when I sat up. Leaning on Alex for support, I hobbled out of the hospital and spent the balance of the day gritting my teeth trying to get comfortable in the face of what was now chronic pain in my abdomen.

That night in my bedroom I reached gently for a book on my nightstand, *What To Expect When You're Expecting.* I had checked it out of the library earlier in the week. I could not bring myself to actually buy the book at the bookstore. It would have been too bold. I'd become very superstitious and decided such a purchase would jinx the outcome of our IVF. I knew, at this point, I was only on the precipice of pregnancy.

Not far into chapter two my eyes grew heavy. Given the surgery, I had to lie on my back in an uncomfortable, almost upright, position, which meant I slept fitfully. There wasn't much I could do that didn't aggravate my abdomen. Writing in my journal didn't require much effort and it was one way to sort out the confused thoughts in my head as we waited for nature – aided by a team of scientists – to take its course during the next two agonizingly slow weeks. While I fretted about whether we would end up with a bun in the oven I wondered how other women had found the patience, the stamina, to face this weird journey. It was just one of the things I wrote about. The other was recording the regular hospital reports:

Day Three – Tuesday: *At 8:15 am we received a call saying that only nine of the eggs were good enough to fertilize. Seven fertilized eggs had proven viable. Of those, two were at the eight-cell stage - Grade 1 (FANTASTIC!); one was at a nine-cell stage - Grade 2; and the remaining four were still at the early dividing stage. They explained that since we had three that looked really good the embryologist felt we were good to go for the transfer today.*

We were in very good spirits when we arrived at the REI clinic – practically giddy with anticipation. The nurse administered a mild dose of Valium to relax my muscles and I felt myself go deliciously limp. Our embryologist stopped by our procedure room with a photograph of the embryos. She described them as "beautiful." Alex was clearly excited and chatted up the embryologist, eager for more information. He asked whether they had played any Barry White music during the fertilization phase to get them in the mood. She laughed and said "No, no Barry White," then appreciating the special nature of her work, she added with care, "but sometimes we do sing to them."

Alex joked that if we had a boy, we'd have to name him baby Stanley in honor of Stanford. Minutes later, Dr Marvelous told us that if he had only the photos to go by he would have believed that they were the embryos of a 27-year-old woman. I was so proud! As soon as my bladder was full, we watched with fascination on the ultrasound as the doctor guided a catheter and placed the growing embryos (or "embies" as I called them) at the top of my uterus. I was now something altogether new and exciting: PUPO (Pregnant Until Proven Otherwise).

Day Five – Thursday: *Relaxed at home per doctor's orders in the afternoon and all day Wednesday -- sleeping intermittently and doing some light paperwork to distract me. We affixed the picture of the embryos to the refrigerator door. Perhaps it's the first photo in the brag book or scrapbook? Midday the embryologist called to tell us that our remaining two embryos had developed to the blastocyst stage and that they were being frozen per our* *wishes. Terrific news! That means we have more chances if for some reason we're not successful with an implantation this time. Even better, they could be siblings in a future cycle. Why not think positive?*

Day Six – Friday: *Went back to the office Thursday afternoon and Friday. Relieved for the distractions that work meetings and projects provide. Felt very confident Thursday and early Friday that something good was occurring inside me.*

Day Seven – Saturday: *Seven days and counting until blood is drawn to determine if we are officially pregnant. Woke up this morning feeling uncertain and not terribly optimistic that implantation occurred. My bloating and breast swelling is down. Trying not to feel let down. Reading as much as I can in the hopes that the more I know the better I can assess the situation. Have had tremendous support from our brothers and sisters-in-law -- very much appreciate their kindness and discretion.*

On Day Thirteen my world turned upside down. My hope for pregnancy began to slip away. My thoughts alternated between resignation and determination. I laced up my sneakers and headed out for a very slow walk around the neighborhood. I gulped the fresh air to try to stop the bombardment of negative thoughts. My agitation returned in force when I arrived home. Alex sat on the porch looking distracted. I greeted him with tears. "I know it's useless to torture myself, but this waiting is killing me."

Alex softly embraced me in a hug. "I know, honey. Neither of us should speculate. It's out of our hands. We'll know tomorrow."

Throughout the rest of the day I felt cramping in my uterus – ominous sensations that something might have gone terribly wrong. By evening I was a wreck and cried myself to sleep. Mercifully I slept through the entire night. I awakened Friday morning and while Alex was still asleep I did exactly what the doctor told me not to do – I peed on an at-home pregnancy test.

The result was all too familiar – one pink line. I refused to give up all hope. I convinced myself that it might simply be too soon for an over-the-counter response. A blood test would be more definitive. On the drive to the hospital my mind wandered, grateful for the distraction of an NPR radio program. I pulled into the familiar hospital parking garage with my nerves on edge. Once I parked the car and climbed out I felt my legs go weak and buckle. I had no choice but to sit back in the driver's seat and brace myself for what lay ahead.

With as much concentration as I could muster I walked slowly up the parking garage stairs and past the water dancing playfully in the fountain just outside the hospital entrance. All around me the normal bustling of the hospital staff belied the life or death blood test I faced. Had the embryos survived? Had they graduated from blastocysts to zygotes? I took the elevator up to the third floor and approached the REI clinic. I saw a woman standing in front of the two closed glass doors.

Oddly, the doors to the clinic were pulled shut and locked. A bad omen if there ever was one. Another woman and I stood on the outside looking in. We had no choice but to wait for someone inside to exit and allow us access. Finally, after a few minutes that felt more like hours, the door opened. The other woman and I navigated the circuitous path back to the lab each carrying our respective lab forms. I fell in line behind her. Two other women arrived immediately after me.

The technician greeted me when it was my turn with a cheerful, calm voice and looked over my form. "Ah, I see you're here for a 'beta' – you're my third today."

The word "beta" hit me like a sucker punch. It dawned on me then just how tenuous the whole IVF process truly was. We'd made it through the "alpha" stage, but there was still a long road ahead of us. Silicon Valley is full of betas – projects under development but not yet in full production. It was one thing if it referred to a software product, it was quite another when it was your child under development – the place between conception and a full blown pregnancy.

Back in the privacy of my car I felt a lump rise in my throat. My eyes filled with familiar tears and I fought back a sob. Again, I had a strong sense that the official outcome would not be a happy one. The next six hours in my office I tried valiantly to distract myself with busy work – phone calls, meetings, and collaborating on projects with colleagues – grateful for any interruption to my heavy thoughts. Alex, working from home, was going through similar motions. At 3:30 I gathered some files and prepared to head home so I could field the nurse's call with the blood test results from the comfort and privacy of our living room. I rang Alex on my cell phone. When I heard his voice I grew hopeful once again. I chattered on about the great outcome of one of my marketing projects and told him I'd be home shortly.

I charged into the house with a full bladder and headed purposefully toward the bedroom and into the adjoining bathroom offering Alex a quick kiss en route. Oddly, he followed me closely. I could sense him hovering outside the door of the bathroom as I located my progesterone suppository. He blocked the doorway preventing me from getting to the bed where I needed to lie down in order to comfortably insert the capsule prescribed after the embryo transfer. This intimately-placed hormone was needed for several weeks while the pregnancy moved from alpha to beta and beyond.

"Some privacy, please," I said with great impatience. "And why do you have that strange look on your face?"

Before I could move another inch he quickly walked toward me and pulled me into a tight hug. He whispered in my ear. "You can forget about the progesterone capsule, Pammie. It isn't needed any more."

Apparently the nurse's call had come in ten minutes earlier while I was driving home. She informed Alex that the blood test result had come back negative. There was, she was sorry to say, no evidence of a beta stage pregnancy.

Alex's words took a moment to register. Hot tears formed in my eyes. I gasped for air trying to regain a sense of equilibrium. I pulled away from him, oddly defiant. He knew instinctively that I needed to be alone and moved quietly to the front of the house. He, too, needed some space. Our much sought-after children, the three embies, only existed now in the grainy black and white photo affixed to the refrigerator door.

He carefully removed the image. He held it for a moment before finding an envelope in which to tuck it away. He knew it would only upset me further if I saw it.

I changed into some comfortable old sweats and stepped into the backyard. A bright yellow Adirondack rocking chair beckoned. I rocked forward and back holding my arms across my still-swollen abdomen and struggled to accept what I had just heard. I wanted so desperately to have a good cathartic cry but all I could muster were some choked sobs and a runny nose. I needed Alex now. I found him inside slumped in a chair, dejected. I offered to make us both a good stiff gin and tonic. We both wanted to be numb. Together we returned to the matching rocking chairs.

"You know," I said, "I had convinced myself in the last mile or so of my drive home that you would greet me with some happy news."

He replied with a heavy sigh. "You have no idea how sincerely I wish that had been the case."

Neither of us could think of anything else to say so we sipped our drinks in silence, the alcohol quickly taking effect, and stared blankly up at the sky. Slowly my tears came and didn't stop. Big tears, drawing from a vast reservoir, flowed silently down my cheeks.

It had been a week since we had learned about the negative test result and a deep depression had fallen over me, slowing my movements and sapping what little energy I had left. The sound of the alarm clock was a rude reminder that I had to try to get on with my life. I dragged my body into the bathroom and caught a look in the mirror. Staring back was a swollen, tear-stained face. My eyes were rimmed in red and the surrounding tissue was alarmingly puffy.

"Lovely," I uttered aloud as I turned the shower on to warm up the water. In just over an hour I was due to meet with a colleague to discuss a new marketing initiative. The warm water running over my still recovering, hormone-bloated body provided a measure of comfort. Back in front of the mirror I futilely applied eye drops to reduce the redness and eye moisturizing gels in an attempt to minimize the puffiness.

In the office parking lot I checked my makeup in the rearview mirror. I knew there was little more I could do to disguise my sadness. Of the twenty-five people in my office I had only told the office manager that I was undergoing treatment for infertility. And I only told her because I needed a legitimate explanation for my constant coming and going down Sand Hill Road to Stanford Hospital. I'd sworn her to secrecy for a few reasons. First, I didn't need the added pressure of colleagues inquiring or involving themselves in inappropriate speculation about my condition. Second, I needed a neutral zone where I could lose myself for hours at a time in projects that didn't involve counting egg follicles and the like. Finally, I didn't want infertility to define me entirely.

I walked into my colleague's office, grateful for the drawn blinds. The sun could be blinding in her office at that time of day. She was hunched over a laptop on her desk and looked up with surprise at my obviously swollen eyes. She paused as though not quite sure if she should inquire about the cause when I mumbled something about bad allergies and immediately launched into a marketing campaign discussion. My colleague followed my lead and pulled out a spreadsheet.

Alex wanted to make it all better for me. He tried his best jokes. He offered back rubs. He arranged to take me out to dinner, a "date night" on a Saturday. We got early reservations at a lively restaurant. All was going pretty well. I was able loosen up some, to find enjoyment in my meal and the bottle of wine we shared. We stuck to conversation topics that didn't require much effort – the latest movie showing at the local theater, the odds of the Michigan Wolverines getting a shot at the national championship that fall. My body started to visibly relax.

My composure began to crumble, though, when a noisy, large party of young women arrived and were seated adjacent to us. Snippets of conversation about morning sickness and labor pains foreshadowed what was to come. The din grew louder as the guest of honor arrived. A glowing young woman easily approaching her ninth month of pregnancy filled the doorway to the dining room. I blanched as the mommy celebration scene unfolded. There was no escaping the spectacle. A few of the other diners joined in the festivities, cooing over the swollen-bellied woman holding

court to offer congratulations and reminisce fondly about their own pregnancies. Once the pregnant woman wedged her way into her seat I made
a beeline for the ladies room and told Alex I'd meet him outside, foregoing
dessert or coffee. The ladies room offered no respite, though.

"Doesn't Piper look marvelous all pregnant?" yelled one woman from
behind the bathroom door to her friend one stall over. "She could pose
on the cover of a magazine like Demi Moore if she wanted! You know I
heard she had some pictures taken in the nude last week."

"I wish I'd taken pictures last year when I was about to deliver. Pregnancy makes you feel like, well, so womanly doesn't it?"

"Totally! Piper looks like her water could break at any time. Hey,
where were you when your water broke?"

This was one time I wished for one of those seriously noisy bathroom
blow dryers to drown out the painful chatter. With my hands barely dry
I bolted from the restroom.

We faced a big question: when to proceed with our two frozen embies, the "twins" resulting from the egg harvest. It didn't make sense to
keep them on ice any longer than they needed to be so I contacted the
nursing staff at the clinic to learn what was involved in the latest fertility
treatment alphabet, the FET – frozen embryo transfer. The nurse explained that I would follow a natural cycle. On or about Day 11 – the
earliest I could expect to ovulate – the plan called for an ultrasound to
check out my endometrial lining. In other words, determine how hospi-
table my womb was to receiving embryos. After one or two ultrasounds
I would get a mega-dose of hormones, in the form of a shot, to induce
ovulation. I would then start my lovely progesterone suppositories twice
a day, and seven days after the big shot, I would come in for the embryo
transfer. The embies would have been thawed that morning. My biggest
assignment on transfer day was to fill my bladder to capacity.

"Got it," I said as I took careful notes. "Well, looking at the calendar, I expect my period in about twelve days. Can we get something on the schedule?"

Much to my surprise the nurse informed me that I'd have to wait a
few months. They had a backlog of women ahead of me awaiting full-

blown IVF treatments, and they were planning to close the lab for a few weeks in August.

"You mean the world doesn't revolve around me?" I asked facetiously.

"No, girlfriend."

In preparation for the next treatment go-round I opted to give acupuncture a whirl. The office where "Dr. Needles" operated was not, thankfully, in the hospital. It was easily accessed right off Sand Hill Road. I was one of the lucky ones. My office was only three miles away from Stanford. I'd often overheard other women lament their long drives to these procedures.

On a late Tuesday afternoon I wrapped up a project in the office. As I made my way to my acupuncture appointment I switched mindsets from Professional Pamela to Patient Pammie. In the treatment room, which resembled those in a spa usually reserved for self-indulgent massages, a nurse handed me a hospital gown to change into. In the dimly lit room soothing music played on a CD. I took some deep breaths and tried to get comfortable on the table. What a welcome contrast to the clinical nature of hospital exam rooms. I remembered seeing Dr. Needles come and go from the REI clinic. He was a soft-spoken man who radiated peace, and here he was.

Whenever a person in a white coat appeared and asked, "What brings you here?" my infertility history tumbled out. As I shared the *Reader's Digest* version, Dr. Needles took notes and nodded respectfully without a whiff of judgment (which I adored him for). Curiously he wanted to inspect my tongue. Apparently tongues do more than taste and help with talking. For more than two thousand years, traditional Chinese medicine, I learned, has relied on the tongue and its color and characteristics for disease diagnosis. Who knew the tongue held such valuable clues? It was amazing the quirky knowledge I gathered out and about on my baby quest. Satisfied and now armed with tongue-centric insights, Dr. Needles reached for his acupuncture needles.

On my back with my head propped up slightly by a soft pillow, I watched as he placed needles in my feet, along my calves, on my thighs, around my belly, in my arm. The last ones went into the crown of my head and around my ears. The needles, he explained, were at "meridian points" where energy traveled through my body. I was not altogether sure what to expect, and while the pricks of the needles were noticeable, they were neither uncomfortable nor painful. He encouraged me to relax for forty-five minutes, adding that sometimes patients actually fell asleep. He left as quietly as he arrived.

My breathing slowed. Calm, restful images drifted through my mind. I imagined I was lying on a lounge chair near an ocean, the sun warming me while a soft breeze caressed my skin. Before I knew it, I drifted into a meditative state – neither asleep nor awake, but completely relaxed. My limbs felt heavy. My mind was completely at peace. In what seemed only a few minutes Dr. Needles was back to remove the needles. This was one doctor I didn't mind seeing as often as needed. We scheduled another five visits, the last of which would take place at the REI clinic on transfer day. He bowed as he left the room while I clumsily attempted to bow back.

I saw Dr. Marvelous for the first in my new series of ultrasounds, as scheduled by the nurse. It was an awkward re-acquaintance. He understood, looking at my records, that I had had a very difficult time accepting the first IVF outcome. The clinic's social worker/counselor had clearly made notes in my file. I felt my face flush. It had been a few months since the clinic shrink and I had met, but it had been a memorable meeting. I sobbed uncontrollably not long after I had arrived for what was supposed to be a get-acquainted session. The appointment took place a few days after our IVF test results. Her kind, soothing voice put me at ease, unleashing an unstoppable torrent of tears. It was the first time I had let loose with my emotions outside of the house and, as my file indicated, it apparently had not gone unnoticed.

Our negative beta hadn't only surprised us; it baffled Dr. Marvelous as well. He shared an analogy which had to do with the engineering concept of "tolerance stack-up." It went something like this: Imagine if each component of an engine (a.k.a our body/organs) was on the outer edge of its allowed variance and was technically acceptable. Nothing was broken, per se. The engine would run, but the sum of those minor imperfections (our combined bio contributions) prevented it (our combined fertility) from ever achieving its full potential. It was a pretty technical description but I found comfort in some type of rationale, even if it evoked images of a badly tuned car. It was certainly better than torturing myself by endlessly retracing every step of the procedure trying to decide where along the way I might have inflicted harm.

As Dr. Marvelous applied gel to my abdomen and prepped the dildo cam with a condom, I tried to make the moment less weird with small talk. I brought him up to date on my acupuncture sessions. Lo and behold, when my uterus came into view on the screen, Dr. Marvelous gasped and marveled as we saw the images take shape. He said he had never seen such a strong response to acupuncture. My endometrial layer was in wonderful condition. My right ovary also carried a beautiful egg follicle. I told him I had two more acupuncture sessions scheduled, including one in the hospital just prior to the transfer. I all but danced down the hall on my way out of the clinic.

On the eve of our transfer I slept fitfully, wishing I could recapture the tranquil state I experienced while under the needles. I awoke at 2:30 in the morning, tossing and turning until 4 a.m. I tried reading in the guest room to distract my overly active mind and finally managed to drift off. When I climbed out of bed at 6:45, I knew it was going to be a bitch of a day. Still, I was not quite prepared for the latest wave of emotions that washed over me.

Alex was already into his first cup of coffee and dressed to go to the gym for his usual Saturday morning pickup basketball game. In front of the TV to record the Michigan game that afternoon he seemed blissfully unconcerned about our 11 a.m. appointment at the REI clinic. Cranky and agitated by progesterone hormones, I went on the attack.

"Nice priorities! Sports are clearly more important to you than worrying about how *I'm* doing?"

He stopped his programming and tossed down the remote. "Pammie, that's not true. I don't have to go anywhere. It's just that I've got lots of nervous energy to burn off."

I burst into tears. "Go! Just get on with your game. I'm not fit for human company anyway."

I was so caught up in my own drama that I'd conveniently overlooked any difficulties Alex had in going the high-tech route to fatherhood. It now occurred to me that basketball was a form of therapy for him. The physical game alleviated his anxiety and his teammates distracted him with inane sports talk. He could push them around on the gym floor to work out his own angst and disappointment. It was a year or more before I learned the extent of his frustrations.

After he left for the gym I poured some orange juice and toasted a bagel so I could take my meds. I scanned the paper without comprehending much. Restless myself, I threw on baggy clothes and headed outside to walk off my anxiety. It was a beautiful, clear late autumn morning. I knew it would be my last sanctioned exercise for some time and I was determined to get it in.

I kicked up the leaves around me and thought about our last embryo transfer. Tears rolled down my cheeks as I recalled the naïve hope I had once held on to so tightly. We'd made it through each of the IVF steps with flying colors and felt sure we would score a pregnancy. I mourned our three little embies. I racked my brain to recall each of my actions in the days following the first transfer. I wanted desperately to know what, if anything, I might have done that could have contributed to their demise so I could avoid a repetition the next time around. I worried about the two embies that were being thawed that morning and wondered if they would survive the procedure. Would they be any stronger than the last three? This time I vowed to do better, to be a better mother to them. The acupuncture was surely going to help, wasn't it?

At the appointed hour Alex and I climbed into Big Shirl for the all-too-familiar ride up the peninsula. This time we were silent. We arrived at a waiting room full of couples and took the last two seats available. I tried hard not to look too interested as my fellow infertiles were called in one by one. We were among the last couples seated when, at 11:30, a nurse called my name. We had spent so much time in the procedure rooms that we had already read all of the old magazines left there. Alex loaded the CD player, as he said, "to set the mood." The room filled with nature sounds and soft instrumentals sounding like harps. Another nurse showed up with a cup of water and a Valium to relax my muscles and, I hoped, my mind.

"Got any for me?" Alex asked, half seriously.

She shot him a sympathetic smile. "Sorry, these only go to the ladies on transfer day. We need you to remain alert and drive her home safely."

"Guess I'm good for something, then," he responded.

The Valium took effect and a welcome calm infused me.

"Alex, honey," I said somewhat groggily. "I'm sorry for snapping at you this morning."

He reached over and took my hand. "Don't worry. I've learned to take the hormone monster in stride."

Dr. Needles arrived. Alex watched with amazement as he carefully inserted the acupuncture needles. Between the Valium and the needles I was floating peacefully without a care in the world, delighted to be transported to what I can only describe as paradise. After twenty minutes Dr. Needles removed the instruments of bliss while Dr. Marvelous informed us that one of the blastocysts looked quite strong and that the other, while not as advanced, was worth transferring as well. Alex and I quietly nodded in agreement. We watched on the ultrasound screen as Dr. Marvelous skillfully inserted a catheter through my cervix and into my uterus. Once in position, he told the nurse he was ready for the blastocysts.

Alex stroked my arm, not removing his eyes from the screen while an embryologist arrived and asked me to state my name. She compared it to the name on the pipette she held cautiously and nodded. These were indeed the right embryos for the right waiting uterus. She turned the precious cargo over to Dr. Marvelous. We watched as he deposited them with the utmost care into my uterus and removed the catheter. After twenty-five minutes in silence the nurse knocked on the door to tell us it was okay to move.

With Alex escorting me like I was an invalid, I walked slowly and delicately into the hallway. I couldn't help but worry that the embies might fall out. As we passed Dr. Marvelous and the embryologist in the hall both forced a smile and wished us luck. That unnerved me a little. We needed more than luck. Seated outside the hospital entrance near the dancing fountain, I waited for Alex to bring the car around and concentrated on living in the moment. I breathed deeply reveling in the sun's warmth and the blue skies overhead. I told myself that *this* alpha pregnancy would take.

The beginning of our two-week wait coincided with Thanksgiving week, which I had arranged to take off. We lounged around the house consuming hour after hour of *The Sopranos*. We had the full DVD set at the ready. Mostly I wanted to be anywhere but inside my head. I lay on the sofa, immobile so as not to push the blasts or myself at such a crucial time.

Every once in a while we talked tentatively about what we hoped was going on inside my womb – not wanting to become too attached but also wanting to dream about the likelihood of seeing a full-blown pregnancy and a bouncing baby (or two!) emerge some nine months later. Dreams of a late spring delivery danced in my head. Ah, yes, managing sleep deprivation during the long and carefree days of summer. One could hope, right?

When I got the official word on the second beta outcome I was stunned. As requested, I had shown up at 8:20 a.m. in the lab, which was buried in the bowels of the old hospital building, for my blood work. How did the poor soul whose job it was to draw blood face such a surreal parade of mostly somber young women every morning? I hoped they provided battle pay to those affiliated with the reproductive endocrinology clinic. During my expeditions to the lab, just one of many pit stops required in the baby-making program, I had witnessed women going off like firecrackers. It wasn't pretty. Neither was the lab, which had as much cheerfulness as a bomb shelter – no windows but lots of gray cabinets and tables and pipettes and glass and plastic tubes.

But I've digressed. My uterus had clearly enlarged over the past week and I had been feeling periodic bouts of nausea, all of which made me smile more than I had in months. The knowledge that this time would be different transformed me. I positively glowed. Even my colleagues remarked on it.

"What gives? You haven't stopped smiling since you got here."

I was not about to share my tentative secret prematurely. On the morning of the blood draw I requested that the REI nurse call Alex with the results since I would be locked in a day-long meeting and wouldn't be near my desk. That was one bit of information I didn't want to hear via voicemail. I decided not to contact Alex ahead of arriving home. On the road home at 5:40 that evening, I prepared myself for the good news. I imagined that Alex had gone out to buy some flowers in celebration. I played out in my mind how wonderful it would be to greet my parents with the good news when they arrived for a Christmas visit in a few weeks time. I felt gloriously nauseous. What more could I ask for? I cranked up the radio and sang along with my favorite tunes while traffic crawled.

Forty-five minutes later I turned the key in the front door lock and walked in quietly. I looked about eagerly for some sign of the news that awaited me. Nothing apparent. Within minutes Alex walked from the back of the house. His face betrayed no emotion. Like when he proposed to me, I wondered if he was playing hard to get.

"So?" I asked.

"I'm sorry, honey," he said quietly. "The result is the same as last time."

I punched him playfully. "C'mon…stop pulling my leg," I said, my face signaling confusion.

He leaned in to hug me. "Really, that's not something I would joke about. I'm sorry."

I continued not to believe. "How can that be? I feel pregnant. I'm sick to my stomach."

"So am I," he responded with no amount of humor.

It just could not be. I was dumbfounded. *If this is what pregnancy is* not *supposed to feel like, then how does the real thing feel?* I shook my head and repeated, "Damn, damn, damn! I really thought we had it this time. What exactly did the nurse say?"

"The hormone level was far too low to signal a valid pregnancy."

Again, utter amazement. "Okay then. I need a glass of wine. Bring the bottle."

In December, on the Saturday evening after our very early miscarriage, a light rain fell as we pulled up to the front entrance of a clubhouse. I hopped out and stepped gingerly through puddles to keep my suede pumps from getting soaked. The office manager from the venture firm where I worked greeted us in the lobby and joyfully herded us and a crush of colleagues into a festively-decorated room reserved for the annual holiday party. Each year the firm pulled out all the stops. As most in our office had little ones, it was a family-themed party – kids were not only welcome, they were indulged.

Inside the room closest to the bar were a handful of young, single employees with their dates or married couples like me and Alex who didn't (presumably "yet") have children. On the other end of the spectrum were the majority – colleagues and their spouses, who brought children and lots of them, ranging in age from a few months old to pre-teens. The venue had an area set aside for activities aimed at entertaining the little ones – decorating gingerbread houses, face-painting, painting ornaments or watching adults dressed as jesters create balloon figures. There were hired childcare providers to keep an eye on the kids so the parents could get some time to socialize and enjoy a well-choreographed gourmet dinner. A challenge for all of the adult merry-makers was running the kid gauntlet, since many of the little ones with frosting and paintbrushes were not content to stay in their designated area. I narrowly dodged one adorable little girl who ran by wielding a cupcake and a plastic cup full of root beer. Coming in the other direction was a conga line of kids hurrying to queue up for their audience with the next entertainer.

It was all I could do to make it through the night without breaking down as colleague after colleague made a point of proudly introducing their children to us. They had no idea of the pain they were inflicting, how I was weeping inside for my lost children.

Days, weeks and months went by, but I could not let go of the idea that our biological children were out there waiting for us. Our move away from all types of treatment was a slow, often circuitous process that sometimes led us back like a junkie in need of a fix to the reproductive endocrinology clinic for one more work-up. We had to try again. Something. Anything. We'd had encouraging responses to treatment. It was an imperative that we keep trying, a need so strong that it was beyond rational explanation. We thought that perhaps if we kept looking we'd find a new factor, a clue we hadn't yet considered or addressed. There were so many tiny interrelated steps need to achieve a successful pregnancy. We just had to crack the code. A voice in my head – or was it my heart? – kept egging me on. Over the next nine months we reverted back to the less expensive IUI for a few cycles, pairing it with acupuncture. I underwent another laparoscopy to clear my womb of any problematic tissue inhibiting implantation. I was thirty-nine and a half when we attempted one more full-blown IVF cycle.

The outcome was no different. Our hard-won embies hopefully nurtured along didn't make it beyond the first two weeks. All the while, the doctors continued to scratch their heads with no definitive explanation for our lack of success, dampening our hopes that we'd ever get pregnant, even with the best the medical world had to offer.

Convinced Stanford was being too conservative, I sought out a notoriously experimental clinic closer to San Francisco. We underwent a new battery of blood tests, which uncovered no new inhibitors. Soon we were in line for a more aggressive IVF, set to take place in the third week of June. All was ready. Alex was a day away from purchasing more ridiculously expensive hormones when the clinic nurse reached me at my desk between meetings. She informed me that we could not proceed as scheduled. Further review of my files indicated that as of June twelfth, I would be forty years old. Protocol, she informed me, required that any patient older than forty first undergo a baseline mammogram.

That's when I lost it. I slammed down the phone.

If my IVF had been scheduled a week earlier they would have proceeded. There was something about this new requirement – a new test that would take another month or so to schedule, conduct and await the results of – that became the straw that broke the camel's back. The very idea that I was now categorized in a high-risk group, forty-plus, well – it shattered me.

More than that, we had seen other people go through double or more the number of IVF rounds without success. We had spent $50,000, with nothing but heartache to show for it. But perhaps the greatest consideration was the realization that losing more IVF offspring was just too much to bear – especially when the rest of the world (minus our immediate family and a handful of close friends) didn't know about or recognize our losses.

We could not cope with another fleeting encounter with our desperately wanted children-to-be. Each embryo created and transferred held such promise. Each complex cycle forced us to say hello and goodbye before we'd ever had a chance to get to properly know each other. We simply could not face another failure and loss on that scale, especially in such a support-deprived vacuum.

"Pammie, this is the right decision," Alex told me one Sunday morning as I sat with a heating pad nursing cramps associated with my period.

"At times I didn't know which was worse," he added, "my own disappointment or watching you get your hopes up and then get destroyed."

WHAT DOES A NON-MOM WEAR WHEN NOTHING FITS?

CHAPTER FOUR

DENIAL: LA, LA, LA, I CAN'T HEAR YOU

While the doctor visits stopped, great expectation lived on. As summer turned to fall I kept buying ovulation and home pregnancy tests, hoping against hope that we'd be the miracle story – the one couple who beat all the odds. What about tapping into that luck of the Irish? My paternal grandfather was an O'Mahony from County Cork and my paternal grandmother was a Green, also of Irish descent.

With no sign of a miracle pregnancy and no more appointments to juggle I spent more and more of my free time wandering around department stores scouting through the clearance racks in search of a "great buy" – it was retail therapy pure and simple. I filled my arms with boat-necked cotton sweaters, low-waisted slacks and the occasional slinky dress, and hung them haphazardly in the fitting room. Peeling my top over my head, kicking off my shoes and abandoning my jeans, I hungrily reached for the next item to try on. If I was going to be infertile I was going to be a "Hottie Infertile," damn it! The one item of clothing permanently banned from my shopping list was the smock top. It had become quite a popular style for non-pregnant women. No matter that it was meant to be whimsical. I didn't want to give anyone reason to wonder if my non-defined waist under the smock top meant I was in the family way. Just the risk of inviting such a question or speculation when I knew it was outside the bounds of possibility was too painful to endure.

Sometimes I bought with gusto, the thrill of the hunt satisfying some strange longing. I unpacked my finds with satisfaction. There was the smart outfit perfect for a lunch with a colleague or a date night with Alex. Other times I found the shopping experience left me empty. It didn't take long for me to see my recent activities in a new light. The metaphor was so obvious as to be clichéd. I had been slowly changing the color of my hair and its style. I'd been trying on different clothes or looks to satisfy a greater urge to literally transform physically into a different person – a *non-mom*.

The problem, so far, was that nothing seemed to fit. Usually in such life-course corrections when a path wasn't clear, the natural instinct was to go with the herd. Only trouble was finding the right one. I was slowly separating from the "Trying to Conceive Tribe" and from the looks of it I wasn't ever going to be part of the "Mother Tribe" – the working mother or the stay-at-home mother set. The schism between the two camps was now so *whatever*. I didn't even fit into the "Childfree by Choice Tribe." I learned a new term. I was "involuntarily childless." How the hell was I going to locate that motley crew?

———

I found Alex at the kitchen table not long after the New Year. It was 2004. He was reading the newspaper, happily enjoying the sports section and remarking on how much he had enjoyed the movie we'd seen the night before. In a matter of minutes, I destroyed his blissful morning. I slowly put down the front page I'd been unsuccessfully attempting to read and tried to relay my thoughts to him, the ideas jumbled and disjointed. Six months had passed since we had ceased fertility treatment.

"You know, I've just realized that my shopping fix has been nothing more than a sorry attempt to disguise myself as a different person."

He threw down his newspaper confused by my *non sequitur* and looked over at me, his brows knit.

"I know it sounds crazy," I said as I stood and began pacing fretfully, "but I spent most of last year floating around. Now I'm pissed and frustrated because I realize I've made no progress.

"I don't know if it's part PMS or early onset mid-life angst. It's just that I'm stuck. I'm lost. I can't seem to find my way. I have another forty good years or more if I'm lucky but, without my own kids and grandkids, I don't know how I'm going to fill them."

Alex did his best to talk to me down from the ledge. "Pam, you're beating yourself up. You've got a lot to be proud of. You're a wonderful daughter, sister, aunt – and on most days – wife. Is it really necessary to torture yourself – and me, too?"

"I guess the words I'm trying to choke out," I said with great difficulty, "is that I never thought I'd have to occupy myself with this particular problem. What hurts most is that I always assumed I'd be consumed at this point in my life with more conventional concerns and distractions: getting kids to soccer practice or figuring out how to prepare a nice table for the holidays, sampling new recipes our kids might actually try instead of the chicken fingers and plain pasta."

And there it was. My dilemma wasn't just about finding the right look or a new job that would make me feel more fulfilled. An identity crisis wasn't the biggest problem I *wanted* to have at this point in my life. I could try on all the outfits in every store in the metropolitan area, but they wouldn't have the outfit I wanted most. It was painful to get to the heart of the matter. Especially after I had tried to convince myself I was ready to get on with my life. I had a career, a few hobbies ranging from hiking, gardening and history to music and, of course, now all the wine I wanted. And I was in a loving marriage with a man who had the longest fuse on the planet – one that I had apparently just lit.

Alex's expression changed from concern to total exasperation. His body tensed. I knew I'd crossed into unfriendly territory. This was just not fair to him. He'd been around this subject one too many times.

"So, are you telling me you see our life as unfulfilling? Is there a *bigger* problem here? Are you looking for a way out?"

I was alarmed at his question. It wasn't the conclusion I wanted him to draw. While relieved at having diagnosed my dissatisfaction, I felt awful for having unloaded on him. There was no way I wanted a divorce, but I could see that he *would* if I kept tormenting him this way.

"No. NO! That's not it at all. It's *you* I want. Maybe if I didn't find you so amazing, I wouldn't care so much that I couldn't give you a child. You would have been such a wonderful father."

"You think that not having a child together doesn't bother me as much as it does you?" he said as he stood up abruptly. "Well it DOES. I had given up my dream of being a father *before* we launched into IVF. Then when it looked like it might happen after all…dammit Pam, I don't want to dwell on it. It hurts way too much."

As he finished his fitful confession he stormed into the garage. Just before the door slammed shut I heard him say something about going to the hardware store.

That's about the time I went underground with my ovulation tracking. I had pregnancy tests stashed in the back of my closet and used them the first sign that I might be a day late. The twenty-eight day cycle took on a torturous new urgency. With 324 consecutive cycles already logged since my first period at fourteen, I knew I only had a few viable eggs left. As the months sped by and I turned forty-two, I started to allow myself to imagine a life not driven by monthly cycles and endless associated vigils. I began to loosen the tight grip on my increasingly fragile dream of getting spontaneously pregnant, of having Alex reach down to listen and feel as our baby kicked inside me, of seeing a baby with my father's clear blue eyes stare up at me from the crib, of nursing a son or daughter and feeling their heavy head doze against my heart or brushing their thick luxurious hair, compliments of my mother. That's where most people think this story ends. Couple tries and tries and tries to have a baby. When they can't they either become selfish hedonists or skip down to the local adoption agency, check out the babies on display, make their selection and go home as one big happy family. Yeah, and don't forget the elves and fairy godmother, right? Wrong. I was in full-on *denial*. I was numb and in no position to make any big decisions especially when, in the case of adoption, another life was involved. Even if babies were freely and readily available (which they were *not*) I wasn't going to risk entering into the equivalent of a rebound relationship. I was going nowhere until I was willing and able to come to face to face with my failure, loss and emptiness.

———————◆———————

Have I mentioned that I'm not accustomed to failure? Not that I was any kind of super achiever, but I was raised to believe that hard work, perseverance and playing by the rules sooner or later paid off. I had never been the smartest one in the classroom or the office but by being tenacious and standing up to challenges I had managed time and time again to rise to places few women before me ever had; it took some moxie and a drive to succeed.

As a student at the University of Michigan I interviewed and was selected for a highly sought-after position as a resident advisor in one of the newly turned co-ed dorms. At the same time, with a full course load, I landed the top leadership spot of a student undergrad organization called the Business Intern Program. It mostly comprised MBA-bound, take-no-prisoner types who wanted a Fortune 100 internship to dress up their resumes. Upon graduation as an English major I managed to outwit a few of my business school counterparts and secured one of the coveted spots in a mother hen program at Dow Chemical Company. Living in small-town Midland, Michigan, and devoting my life to polyurethane or ethylene oxide wasn't my cup of tea. So, within a year I packed my bags and headed back to the Motor City.

The auto industry when I joined it in the late 1980s was male-dominated, to put it mildly. It was not unusual for me to be the only woman in a room full of men. They didn't intimidate me in the least. Not long after joining Chrysler I asked the Vice Chairman in an employee town hall meeting how he could explain, in 1990, the dearth of women in senior management in the company and what he planned to do about it. It was a bold thing to challenge an executive who lived on the "Fifth Floor" of the K.T. Keller Building. The Fifth Floor was also known as Mahogany Row, the epicenter of company headquarters, where it was common to catch sight of company CEO and Chairman Lee Iacocca. A male colleague working closely with the Vice Chairman told me that of all the questions he had received – ranging from the company's still-wobbly financial status to our manufacturing changeover plans – he was most put off by yours truly, the "uppity woman" who had the temerity to question the company's hiring and promotion practices.

I didn't mind being the underdog because it allowed me to prove the naysayers wrong. I threw myself into underdog projects with zeal. I enjoyed the intellectual challenge and creativity involved. My hard work paid off. Within seven years I had become familiar with the insides of the corporate jet and I became one of the rare women who made bonus roll, the executive level, at Chrysler Corporation. It came at the same time I was wrapping up a master's degree in Organizational Communication, and waiting for my divorce to be final. To complete the degree required taking classes at night in downtown Detroit in a part of the city that had a higher than normal crime rate. I was undeterred.

When I arrived in Silicon Valley in 1996 armed only with my auto industry experience (like *that* was relevant), I had to take a few steps back career-wise to assimilate and prove myself in this strange new land. I was again the odd woman out in a world dominated by engineers, scientists and bean counters. It was not easy sledding to get technical types to respect or value the marketing or communications functions. Oh, and again, female types in positions of management were more the exception than the rule even in one of the more enlightened industries based in progressive California. Again, undeterred.

Yet against this backdrop of early career success I was reminded every twenty-eight days that in one very important area I had been a total failure. One irony in particular stands out during my early attempts to get pregnant. In 1998 I was on a plane returning to Silicon Valley from Davos, Switzerland, where I had been part of a small team accompanying our CEO to the World Economic Forum. I reached into my briefcase to consult a calendar to figure out when my next ovulation was due to occur when it hit me. In Davos there had been many discussions about the challenges facing future generations. My concern at that very moment was more basic: would I ever be capable of creating life? Would there even be a next generation in my little family to nurture and protect?

Like water eroding stone, my inability to get pregnant – something that came so easily to others – wore me down. I was accustomed to taking my lumps or swimming upstream to get where I wanted to go, but no amount of effort or money – or connections for that matter – had helped to change our reproductively-challenged situation. Infertility clobbered me and my psyche. It forced me to confront a cold hard truth – my womb would likely be forever empty. That realization pounded me into the ground with the force of an anvil. I was – for the first time in my life – deterred.

Worse still, I lost my moxie and along with it my sense of who I was and what my life was supposed to be like. I was in unchartered territory. I had no role models, no Helen Reddy or Mary Tyler Moore theme song to propel me forward. Little by little my professional life had suffered accordingly. How could it not? I had been, well, a little distracted. Furthermore my self-confidence had taken a beating. Not only was I no longer interested in fighting for the next promotion, I didn't think I had what it took to be successful anymore. When one of the managing partners asked me to consider creating a new position working with universities to build relationships with faculty and their most promising, entrepreneurial post-docs, I mulled it over, trying to get excited about a new opportunity.

"So," he asked me when we met again. "What did you decide?"

"I don't think it would be right for me."

"Why is that?"

"First, I think it will be hard to gain respect in a degree-centric community without a Ph.D. but ... well, I just think I'm not the right person. I don't I think I would succeed."

"I could argue the first point, but if you're convinced you'd fail, then that's reason enough not to move forward."

Instead, for the first time in my life, I opted to run in place. I'd do the same, safe work I'd done the past five years. That in itself felt suffocating. Where did one go when the life you had been planning becomes nothing more than a mirage? Those who *could* conceive lived life to a large degree on autopilot with many of life's milestones neatly laid out: marriage, first pregnancy, first baby shower, baby's first words, first tooth, first Halloween, first day of school, first tooth fairy visit, first puppy love, first date, first driver's license… and the list goes on. With clearly anticipated milestones came a set of life plans, actions and reactions. While there were course corrections and bumpy roads to be sure, there was comfort in knowing (generally) what lay ahead and, if all went well, someone would most likely be there to help in the twilight years.

We infertiles, meanwhile, found ourselves trapped in a wickedly confusing "trying to conceive" maze. There were no clear, well-marked paths. Just lots of dead ends. Occasionally we'd stumble across a road marker but it more often than not led us into a cul-de-sac: the first doctor's appointment followed by the first diagnostic test followed by random acts of infertility treatment. Two weeks of hope followed by a week or more of worrying and then defeat. Back to the starting line to try again. Even the minor successes with IVF weren't cumulative. Fertilized eggs that became embryos didn't always lead to babies. Back into the dreaded *cul-de-sac*.

Some of us ran out of gas, and once the infertility treatment road trip to hell ended, there was the decision about how to navigate the future, what new path to choose – most of which came with their own wandering twists, hairpin turns and dead ends. Yes, I know what you're thinking. Look at the bright side, right? Aren't there just as many advantages to plotting one's own course outside the beaten path? Yes, but it also meant getting lost more often. For the nearly ten years we tried to conceive I often felt that I was idling in neutral while my fertile friends and colleagues took off, map in hand, on a mostly pleasant ride. Even when things got rough there were plenty of pit stops for a chance to compare notes with fellow parental road warriors.

I'm not so naive as to believe that parenting is all fun, games and sunshine, but for those of us left eating dust, it was often hard to summon the energy to make the next turn. You see, while there were no guarantees that children would bring happiness to each parent's life, the odds were pretty darned good based on all the reports I'd heard. I'd be a very wealthy woman if I had a dollar for every time I heard some variation on the following statements: "My life's greatest accomplishment is raising my kids" or "I never truly had purpose or meaning in my life until my kids came along" or "When all else is bad in my life, I can look at my kids and feel good."

Implicit in those words was the notion that those without children somehow led less meaningful lives. That not-so-subliminal message wasn't exactly something to cheer about. The devil on my shoulder whispered in my ear: *No matter, you never got the pompoms anyway, remember? You're still the awkward girl who couldn't fit in.* The angel on my shoulder countered: *Okay, so what did we learn oh so long ago? You're smart. You have other gifts. You can prove them wrong. You can live a good life.*

That may be, but first I needed to get *un*-lost, take my mind off of what felt like driving in circles. Meanwhile, our fifth wedding anniversary rolled around (tenth if you counted all our years together). While eloping in mid-February had seemed like a good idea at the time, I later came to regret that our anniversary fell smack in the middle of winter break. Why? Because today's affluent society was perfectly at ease booking winter getaways for the whole family. Not only were rates higher than usual, but the pools, beaches and ski resorts were chock full of screaming children fighting everything from jetlag to the dreaded sugar buzz.

Their parents, accustomed to the noise and intrusion, sat idly by with their iPods or double martinis while their progeny ran around disturbing everyone else. I don't know about you, but when I was the kid (and a very well-behaved one at that) my parents *wanted* time away from us, or at a minimum, a night out at a nice restaurant free from the responsibility of being parents. My parents happily left us with grandparents or a babysitter and some frozen Swanson chicken. And nice restaurants, as a rule, frowned upon noisy rambunctious children tearing about.

Those days were no longer – just like seeing kids riding bikes or walking unaccompanied to and from school. Do you have any idea how hard it was (and still is) to locate a resort that didn't welcome children? We had to leave the country – literally – to find a place where we could be assured that the romantic getaway we had in mind wouldn't be spoiled by someone else's out-of-control kids. (FYI: Resorts in the U.S. are legally barred from discriminating against children, whereas Mexican, Caribbean or European resorts are free to advertise that children under eighteen are not welcome.)

Away from the day-to-day routine a different kind of reality set in. It was a bit of a shock to realize how much of my time and thoughts had been consumed with trying to conceive now that I was no longer "in treatment." For nearly a decade – outside of fulfilling obligations for my day job – organizing doctor visits and monitoring day-to-day cycle changes, reading and sampling ways to improve my odds, combating infertility had been a second occupation. My life had been, in every sense, on hold.

Hang on – where's that music coming from? Don't you hear it?

Okay. *Now* I got it. It was hold music. It had become so familiar that I had tuned it out. Enough! Now turn it off. The muzak began playing with the decision to start our family and against that annoying soundtrack we did what most people do – we factored in the children:

- Let's buy this house! It's in a neighborhood with the best public schools.

- Oh, I can't take that promotion – it's not parent-friendly.

- We'd like to take that extended trip but we really should start a college fund – it's only a matter of time before the babies arrive, and everyone tells us education is getting ridiculously expensive.

- I'd really like to get that sporty two-seater, but where would the car seats go?

For infertiles, it's amazing how many aspects of our lives get shaped around an outcome that may *not* actually happen. I had adjusted my expectations bit by bit as we made more and more discoveries about our inability to conceive spontaneously, but children remained a guiding force in planning our lives nonetheless. Endless tests, prods and treatments later, and little by little my life became all about overcoming infertility ... for the children:

- Now don't forget you can't be out of town on these dates. I'll be ovulating.

- The treatments are going to cost HOW MUCH? And it's all out of pocket? Well, we can cut back on discretionary spending and tap into the college fund to pay the, *gulp*, tab.

- I can't take that exciting job. It will own me body and soul. I need flexibility for the treatments. We just can't risk it.

- Sorry, we'd like to join you but we're sort of tied up with, uh, some scheduling conflicts.

- Honey, you know we can't plan more than a few weeks out. We're at the mercy of the clinic's scheduling.

- We have to cancel hosting the Thanksgiving dinner at our place. I'll be in the post-embryo transfer waiting period. The doctors explicitly said I can't push myself.

- I'm kind of emotionally exhausted. I don't want to think about what comes next.

- Can't we just "be" for a while? I don't want to think about life without children.

- *Sigh.* I get it. There won't be any children.

It was just so difficult to disconnect entirely. Infertility was like *Waiting for Godot*. There was the ever-present waiting, waiting, waiting. Who knew my thirties would become the lost decade? Knowing what I know now, I'd like to petition the universe to refund that time and money. I'd like to rewind so I can retroactively redirect my life without the children. Preparing indefinitely for an outcome that infertility hijacked threw me for a loop.

I felt like a prisoner being released after a long sentence. I hardly knew how to act. While in my early forties I still looked and felt young. I even got carded while wearing a tank top, jean shorts and flip flops. I had a trim figure with perky boobs (one advantage to never having breast-fed) with presumably a lot of life left to live. So what to do? I could rationalize. Okay, what have we got? Surely there are some silver linings in this gloomy-ass cloud. Let's see. No school schedules will dictate our vacation time. No need to accumulate special savings for a college fund. Surely we could make our new-found independence work for us. A mid-life career change perhaps? Yeah, but that required energy and I was fresh out of it. Zapped.

My wounds were still too raw. That damage was going to take some time to repair. Living carefree was not an option – that, too, would require lots of energy because I'd have to do so much *pretending*. Outside of putting one foot in front of the other, there was now only one way for me to cope. In addition to hiding behind denial, I turned off my emotions. I ceased to feel.

Not long after the explosive episode in the kitchen with Alex I withdrew into myself. It lasted for the better part of a year. I can't describe how I managed because I'm not sure how I did. I went through the motions, sleep walking if you will. More babies were conceived and delivered in our extended families, to our friends, and around our neighborhood and the office. The pregnancies and deliveries didn't fully register because I was dead inside. I functioned somehow at a brainstem level. Hermitville. I'd have grown a beard if I could.

What a long way I'd drifted from my days as the dorm social-committee co-chair and neighborhood association board member. There used to be no event too small to celebrate with friends and neighbors – even Groundhog Day or St. Patrick's Day. Why not organize a party? Heck,

Flag Day was great for rum punch, and sangria was perfect on Bastille Day – so refreshing! But who needed holidays as an excuse? Sometimes we'd just reach into our cocktail guide for "Drink of the Week" gatherings. Where once I indulged my extroverted tendencies – initiating conversations with strangers – now I avoided people, strangers and non-strangers alike, so as to avoid the kid conversations whenever and wherever possible. My social isolation intensified, as those closest to me didn't know how to respond. Their platitudes and cheerful assurances that my "turn to be a mom would happen one day" stopped coming. I was a pariah again but this time not because of anything I'd done, but because of what life had served up. No one in our social circle, especially those who had birthed multiple babies (the notion of the "oops babies" being the hardest to stomach), was quite sure what to say or do. There's simply no how-to etiquette on this topic. It was and is a taboo subject.

There's a reason why many people don't talk about it. I've had ample time to observe, like an anthropologist, how people respond broadly to infertility and its treatment – both in my professional world and society at large. Most view infertility treatment, at best, as little more than an expensive and self-indulgent gamble. They assess it no differently from a Super Bowl poll – did the couple win or lose? If they lost, the sentiment is typically, "Well, better luck next time. Hey, there's this great new restaurant that serves tapas. Have you heard about it?"

At worst, the observers cluck their tongues in pity, offering empty platitudes about how "these things happen for a reason." (They don't. Things happen randomly.) Or they draw the conclusion that you somehow earned it. Take your choice: Pity or hostility – I'm not sure which one was more damning.

It's also why I avoided all but the minimum disclosure with my parents. They lived in a different world where couples didn't talk about those ultra-private experiences. And when I did tread into the unspeakable territory, it was hard for them to know how to relate. The only couple they knew in the sixties who had acknowledged any difficulties getting into the "family way" went straight to Catholic Social Services and adopted.

One Christmas they were a childless couple, the next year they weren't. Closed adoptions were hush-hush in those days. One simply didn't pry.

"Maybe it's just the way it was meant to be, Pam," my mother said trying to be helpful as she shook potato chips into a bowl on a summer afternoon in San Jose.

"That doesn't make it any easier, mom." I said as the screen door slammed behind me.

Being in the company of those who didn't know anything about our circumstances was excruciating for a different set of reasons. Small talk about children was (and is) a constant. Lurking out there was the inevitable question, so what about my children? When the question came I had to control my first instinct: letting loose with a blood-curdling scream. Instead I would hide behind a simple but deceptive answer that disguised everything I'd been through. The exchange usually went like this:

"How many children do you have?"

"Ummm...none."

"Oh. Well you are soooo lucky! Say, do you want my kids this weekend?"

And with that my infertility was swept aside, displaced by an inquiry regarding an appetizer or some other frivolity.

Yeah, maybe I was throwing myself a bit of a pity party, but it pretty much sucked to be me for a while. I developed contempt for my body that drove me to ask my ob/gyn for a birth control pill kit that would leave me with only four abbreviated periods a year rather than the customary tear-inducing, failure-mongering dirty dozen. I kept those powerful birth control pills close at hand in the medicine cabinet as a reminder that I still possessed some control. The pills were my way of saying "Okay, you good-for-nothing plumbing, you may have cheated me out of Mother Nature's intentions, but I can shut you down altogether with just a glass of water and this hormone-packed pharmaceutical."

In truth, I couldn't bare the idea of ingesting more hormones. And deep down I wanted desperately to believe a miracle was still possible. My age on paper sounded old but I was still fit and otherwise young-looking. The primal urge to conceive stoked by hope was not something that could be switched off easily. Those birth control pills remained in my medicine cabinet long after they expired. They were one of an odd collection of items I squirreled away from those darker days.

As the weeks went by I wondered how well my painted-on smile successfully masked the depth of my distress. Sometimes I thought the pain was beyond obvious. I felt at times like an inferior actor who overcompensated with big gestures and overdone expressions to try to cover up dramatic deficiencies. I consoled myself with the idea that if I stuck to the "I'm fine" script, those observing me would blindly accept my act. Other days I wanted desperately for them to read the sadness in my eyes. One thing was certain: the people in my day-to-day life were clearly not a discriminating audience. They were too easily fooled into believing that a smile really could erase the gut-wrenching ache I felt, that I was "over" whatever had been mysteriously been keeping me distant at best, or in a bad mood at worst.

I, too, was under the mistaken impression that my wounds had healed. It had been nearly two years since we stopped all medical treatment.

Denial worked as long as the emotional triggers were safely out of reach. During one particularly bad week, the triggers were everywhere. I started to feel again, in the extreme. Sadness and anger wrought havoc on me. All of a sudden I wanted to lash out at the world around me. I had spent the past week or more reading headlines about the unspeakable horror and suffering of families losing children in an overseas earthquake and tsunami. I was strangely drawn to the coverage in the newspapers and on television. I read about the grief-stricken father who said with absolute resignation that his life was over. He had nothing to live for without his son.

In early January 2005 I listened and watched as on-camera journalists fought back their own tears while they pointed out parents walking zombie-like holding the teddy bears of their lost children. The coverage cut to another scene of a mother wailing uncontrollably over the small lifeless body held tightly in her arms. Likewise, my eyes burned with tears as the journalists tried to characterize the depth of loss and unimaginable pain. The television camera panned a row of tiny coffins and my body shook with sobs.

I gasped for air and rocked gently back and forth. I felt a knot tighten in my stomach, and in my mind flashed the scene when I learned that the last two of our seven valiant embryos – *my* hope for the future – died. The sensation of agony and loss was as real for me as I sat watching the news as it had been that sorrowful afternoon, when the phone call from the hospital relayed the news that our final embryos hadn't made it. Our children-to-be – nurtured into existence, if only fleetingly, and depicted in grainy black and white ultrasound images – were as real to me as the children shown in the photographs clutched in the hands of bereaved parents on the television.

I realized pain was not something one could compare or measure or put a value on. I also knew in my heart that my ache was no more or less than that felt by those who had actually nursed a child, changed a diaper or experienced the tender kiss of their child. Yet in a twisted way I envied what they had had. They had felt that magical moment when their baby kicked in the womb. They'd had the joyful experience of seeing their newborn baby open its eyes for the first time. Those were memories they would always have. They were sensations denied me and all the other couples who for whatever reason lacked the biological ability to carry and deliver their own baby.

The survivor's pain was huge, but so, too, had been their joy. I and my infertile sisterhood had experienced only the pain. The tsunami survivors grieved freely and publicly and those around the world poured out their sympathy and understanding. I, along with those in my infertile society, suffered largely in silence with the greater world unaware of – or simply indifferent to – the pain carried about by those of us in their midst. Depending on their age or circumstances the survivors might or might not be able to have more children, but they had had them once. They also had a compassionate societal support structure that acknowledged and supported their mourning. That support structure didn't exist for those whose wombs and arms remained always and forever empty.

I wrapped up a few projects in the office one Friday afternoon. As the sun dipped lower in the winter sky more bliss-filled pregnancy talk filled the hallway. The chatter drifted into my workspace. It surrounded me like poisonous gas. It constricted my airways. I literally gulped for air. I felt my heart pound. One of the guys was chatting up the admin staff about his wife's recent ultrasound. He triumphantly shared his news: A baby boy was on the way. He basked in the attention of the women who were delighted to have an excuse to leave their desks to share in his pregnancy riff. In an increasingly loud voice, he rattled off names that he and his wife were considering for the little nipper.

"I love the name Christopher – doesn't that sound great?"

"Oh, yes!" came the chorus of office staff.

"We can't agree on any names yet," piped up one of the other younger staffers who herself was newly announced and through the first trimester.

I softly closed my office door hoping to block out the noise around the corner. It promised to be another unbearably long six months. More than twenty babies had been born since I joined the firm. I knew I had to accept more mommy- and daddy-to-be talk but it was more than I could take at the moment. It was close to five, time to call it a day and escape before the conversation moved closer to my end of the hallway. I gathered up my purse and jacket and made a quick, unobtrusive exit.

On the weekend I walked through an exercise room mulling over the tragic intersection of those who had lost and created children in such dramatically different circumstances. I looked at the diversity of people going through their routines. There were chubby people in baggy clothes, young buff bodies in spandex toning their abs, and older types on treadmills. The only thing they had in common was an iPod-induced trance. *How many of them are infertile?* I wondered.

From a distance everything about me appeared to be fine. I was outwardly in good health, so why would my insides be any different? The voice inside my head all but screamed out: "*Can't you see my suffering?*"

Was it noble to walk around in pain? To have heartache so pervasive it clung to you wherever you went, regardless of how you tried to escape it? Or was it just plain stupid? Those questions plagued me. Why? No miraculous stork was on its way. Hope had left the building. What remained was the monthly reminder of my broken female bits.

I felt like a mutant, a depressed mutant. There were pharmaceuticals that could take the edge off. At least that's what the magazine and television ads had me believing. But the idea of taking any more pills, even anti-depressants that might dull my pain, was just too distasteful. I decided I was a masochist. I would muddle through, try to deal with my pain on my own. I had to get on with it.

Little did I know then that getting on with it meant moving from a state of numbness to living in a prolonged state of anger. What was the right metaphor to describe how I felt? Sort of a cross between an amputee who had the sensation of phantom limbs, and a caged, wounded lioness. I missed my cubs but no one even knew that they had existed, even as ephemerally as they had. They had once represented a large part of my future but they were gone, never to return.

CHAPTER FIVE

ANGER: TAKE YOUR PREGNANT BELLY AND GET OUT OF MY FACE

(Warning: This chapter contains big time bitterness, bile really)

The anger bubbled up inside me in an ugly way. My world went from Technicolor to black and white. With the end of my baby dreams I started to hate pregnant women. They all seemed to possess a weirdly imperious look. I hated their offhanded way of shopping in the grocery store with their full bellies separating them from the cart. I hated the way they wore form-fitting clothes that all but screamed "I'm growing a baby under here." I hated the way they elicited sympathy from everyone around them and more often than not played the pregnancy condition to their advantage. I hated most of all the way they acted as if it were no big deal that they were carrying life around inside of them. They all seemed to mock me. To me the state of pregnancy was a magical thing not to be taken for granted. It was the complex but carefully orchestrated effort of cells all capable of working together to create a noisy rambunctious boy or a sweet rosy-skinned girl. It was anything but easy and certainly not something that would ever elicit smugness from me.

Did uber-mommies get under my skin? You bet your maternity underwear they did.

And like the drive to reproduce, mine was a primal kind of angry: Me infertile. You fertile. (By the way, this might come as something of a

103

newsflash to *non*-infertiles, but many infertiles view the world through the lens of a fairly strong divide: "infertiles" and "fertiles.")

Is it any wonder? Until I experienced infertility firsthand I hadn't given the notion much thought. I vaguely remember the days when I freely talked about the kind of mother I'd be, the kind of children I'd have. Even in the worst of my trying-to-conceive days I never harbored any hostility toward single people or couples who talked about their future children. That's because I was like them once. Like them I saw my fertility as a given. It was easy to talk a good game when you truly didn't know any better about the whole pregnancy and delivery thing. That's because we were all programmed to think children were inevitable – something to be prevented even. We were reproducing machines.

So how did I feel about those who did know better? Those who had actually experienced the miracle of natural conception? Those who had seen their child's heartbeat on the ultrasound machine for the first time? Those who joyfully bragged about their fertility or virility in ways large and small? They were a different story. I held them to a higher standard and more often than not they let me down – in a big way. Already crushed under the knowledge that I would always be on the outside looking in, I channeled my blackest ire in the direction of fertiles, because they were the ones who should have had the most compassion for those who couldn't conceive. Where they had experienced joy, my counterparts and I experienced devastation. They had bonding and cooing. We had emptiness and silence.

When it became clear that I wouldn't be like the vast majority of other women checking the boxes on the standard life cycle events checklist, I developed something of a fortress mentality and, while digging my moat, I not surprisingly discovered and developed a new form of self-protection. The lines were clear. Infertiles: my allies. Fertiles: my sworn enemies.

It happened slowly. With each negative pregnancy test and failed cycle, I came to view the army of baby-makers with suspicion, dread, and yes, finally, hatred. And they made it so damned easy to hate as they grew more and more smug, with books like *Yummy Mummy* at one end of the spectrum and *Misconceptions* at the other. Speaking of which, I arrived home from work one evening in a particularly bad mood (surprise, surprise). With the best of intentions, Alex mentioned that he had recorded a show he thought would help me – you know, put me in a better mood (hope, hope). It had just the opposite effect.

After dinner he tuned in TiVo and selected a talk show featuring Naomi Wolf. Minutes into the show she outlined the premise behind her book, *Misconceptions*, and the unspoken hardship of being a mother – the hormone swings, the difficulty breastfeeding, how *lonely* being a mother is. Well, I'm here to tell you the television almost got it.

Two minutes into the interview I started yelling at the television screen. *How about NOT being able to be a mother if you really want to know how lonely feels, you bitch! How about the loneliness of being surrounded by a roomful of adults with their children? How about the loneliness of standing in your spare bedroom holding clothing for an infant who, for some unknown reason, just won't come? How about the loneliness of season after season looking at circulars advertising kid's toys or back-to-school outfits or Halloween costumes, and wondering if you'll ever have the need to buy them?*

How about the loneliness of sitting on your toilet while you pee streams of blood month after month? How about the loneliness of waiting in an examining room for yet another lab technician to probe your insides? How about the loneliness that comes with wondering if anyone will come to visit in your old age?

You want to talk about hormone swings? How about voluntarily getting shot up with them twice a day while your abdomen and thighs get covered in black and blue bruises?

Let's just say Naomi and I didn't hit it off. Before I started spitting nails or breaking anything, Alex swiftly deleted the episode and handed over the remote only after I promised not to throw it at him.

"Daddy as dynamo" articles even appeared in the likes of *Details* magazine. That's right – a men's magazine known as a watchdog of style and culture was now carrying stories about how fathers were demonstrating their power and wealth through their virility, by having multiple children. One article noted: "Not only does it show that you have the fertility chops to produce a big family and the fiscal chops to support it, but it also says you're nurturing. It's an upper-class trifecta," said one boastful interviewee.

(*Like my people need another reason to feel like second-class citizens denied admission to the parenting tribe – now we get to feel unhip, too. Oh, and tell me this next guy doesn't have inadequacy, insecurity and a bunch of other issues.*)

"I can't be in a house that only has three kids," Ari says. "The silence scares me. Three kids is so weak. It doesn't feel like you have any."

Where's the justice in these loony tunes filling up spare bedrooms simply because they can, not because they're interested in being responsible parents?

Excuse me while I barf.

Yes, my fertile counterparts became more and more alien to me. They seemed to conceive so effortlessly, even surprising themselves with the power of their own fertility – "He just has to look at me and bam, I'm knocked up!" As a result, I found myself on constant surveillance for pregnant women and their related chatter so I could avoid enemy fire. Sometimes, though, they snuck up on me. There was one day in the office when I came smack into contact with a colleague nearly seven months pregnant, all belly and smock-topped with her second. A cavalcade of emotions ensued, morphing from panic (*not another pregnant belly!*) to anger (*why her and not me?*) and then to resignation (*'cause that's just the way it is*).

I suddenly became very aware of her and my next move. She was engaged with another colleague in an animated conversation about something to do with a school board's indecision. I bristled. There was something about her indignation and how the indecision would adversely affect her child – supported by my taxes by the way – that left me cold. I immediately started casing the joint for an escape while at the same time fabricating a comment should I be asked for an opinion, most of them too sarcastic to actually utter aloud. It became apparent that they were too wrapped up in their parent-centric conversation to notice me. I was able to make a clean getaway.

That's about the time I coined the term "Momzilla" -- or at least I thought I did. It was over the holidays and I was caught in a hair salon smelling of sweet and noxious hair care products, between two women who would not stop talking about the wonders of pregnancy and motherhood. I begrudgingly understood that mommy talk happened a lot where women hung out. I usually did my best to tune them out. This particular incident, though, was far from normal hair salon chit chat. It started between a bubbly, very pregnant hairstylist and her super-happy mommy client, Willow. There I sat amid the faux evergreen decorations draped in a poncho with my hair soaking wet, half of it held back by a clip, a woman standing behind me holding sharp shears. It was a good thing my stylist had a good grip on those shears because I fantasized about sticking sharp objects in the eyes of the two Momzillas.

At first I thought they were joking around – putting the rest of us on with their over the top, "what about the first time the baby kicked?" "The cravings?" "The first time the baby pooped?" "Pregnancy sex, the glow..." It got so bad I had to wonder what I had done to get the universe so intent on torturing me. Even my own stylist, normally unflappable, caught my eye in the mirror and said quietly, "Enough already, huh?"

I have a hunch that Momzillas will always manage to send me into lunar orbit. That would be because they are the Marie Antoinettes of mothers. They are among those who assume that, of course, *anyone* can get pregnant if they really, really wanted to "just look at me!" and if they couldn't, well ... "let them eat cake – with a double non-fat caramel macchiato."

Momzillas seemed to be a dangerous strain of stay-at-home moms. They reminded me of advantaged kids in the affluent community not far from where I grew up who got everything handed to them on a silver platter. They could torment others in the most insidious ways. There they went with their designer duds, pushing top-of-the-line over-engineered strollers to a hip restaurant to lunch with their equally spoiled and insufferable Mommy-and-Me set. I could almost hear Janis Ian singing her famous hit *At Seventeen*:

"I learned the truth at seventeen
That love was meant for beauty queens . . .
Who married young and then retired . . .
(with of course this modified line)
And murmur vague obscenities
At infertile girls like me... "

Persecution complex? Guilty as charged. Ugh. When did I get so touchy? Was it the residual effect of shooting up hormones? After the all-too-often Momzilla encounters I usually required something of a re-set – a "walk it off" moment in the form of aerobic exercise to burn off steam or to summon endorphins. On an exercise bike I'd try to lose myself in *People* magazine – that was until *People* started masquerading as *Parenting* magazine.

What filled the pages? Baby bump watches. Pregnancy announcements. Baby shower gift guides. Baby name speculation. Blow-by-blow delivery stories. Enough! Give me back the gossip magazines of old. Where's Bjork? I longed for days when fashion snafus on the red carpet and stars on their exotic vacations filled the covers. Give me Barbra Streisand as political commentator. Where were the gossip mags that offered the pure, unadulterated joy of escaping the more predictable workaday world that didn't involve parenting tips?

What the ?? One article leaped off the page. It was an interview with actress Keri Russell called, "Five Things I Learned About Being a Mom." Before I knew it I was translating in my head, trying to convert my disgust with yet another cult-of-mommy story into something more palatable. Laughter is the best medicine, right? My more absurd, modified read also showed that we infertiles shared a few more things in common with moms than I once thought. Here's how the altered piece (with infertile substituted for mom and so on) reads, along with my commentary:

Five Things I Learned About Being an Infertile

1) I thought before that you would be diagnosed infertile and you would instantly be like, "I'm an infertile!" But I still feel like a kid. I didn't anticipate that. I have this infertility but I'm the exact same! (*You nailed it Keri! I totally feel like a kid, too! In fact since kids don't factor into my schedule I can indulge in kid-like behavior whenever the spirit moves me. Sometimes I feel like Peter Pan.*)

2) You can't control things like you used to, and you have to roll with things better. (*Wow, I guess we do share more things common than I thought! I had to cede control, too, to the 28-day cycle watch, the demanding prescription drug schedules, and the never-ending two-week waits.*)

3) You still have to see your friends, but the one thing that changes is you have to develop weird bedtime rituals ... so that kind of exes out the dinners with them. (*So true! Sex on demand can sort of throw a monkey wrench into planning —"Excuse us, the ovulation predictor kit says we need to get it ON **right** now"...*)

4) You can't wear nice clothes. But none of that stuff matters as much anyway. There's something else that's so much more important. (*Okay, she was referring to projectile vomiting, which is not altogether unfamiliar to infertiles — I threw up plenty of times after the anesthesia wore off ... and my nice clothes-shopping was curtailed when I had to stop discretionary spending so we could save for treatments that weren't covered by insurance.*)

5) You just become that much more empathetic, and your heart is that much bigger. It's wild, but it happens. (*Yeah, Keri, I know what you mean. I'm much more empathetic now to the loss and pain that infertility brings into relationships, life planning and getting through the holidays...*)

Some could argue that I risked wholly or primarily defining myself as an "infertile woman." My response: society already did that work for infertiles. We never had a choice in the matter. Day in, day out, countless references from others established "fertility" as a key component of their identity. If I correctly recall a lesson from my Marketing 101 course, the net effect is that one positions oneself by positioning the other guy, e.g., "There are credit cards. And there's American Express." Hmmm, which is supposed to be superior?

References to pregnancy and fertility came at me all day long – in the grocery store, the workplace, the airport, on television and in media of all kinds. If infertiles matched example for example with references to our infertility, the fertile world would appreciate how discreet we truly were when it came to not discussing the personal events going on in our world.

Out of curiosity I once tried to count how often I heard or read the expression "as a mom..." but the frequency made it far too hard to keep track. I did a Google News search of "as a mom" which brought back nearly 200 articles in *one* month alone. One article used the description and its variant, "as a mother," three times. Now granted it was an article about juggling parenthood and a profession, but the point stands. The same news search for "as an infertile" brought back zero news articles.

The same exercise applied in real life could net plenty of "as a mom" substitution opportunities. Now, before anyone starts protesting that we can't go around censoring ourselves to the point of neutering our lives, the following examples, from conversations overheard in just one day in the office, simply make the point that a lot of fertility positioning goes on every day. Where you see the words infertile or infertile woman, they are substitutions for the real words used, which were: 1) pregnant 2) mom 3) pregnant 4) mom 5) a mom.

1) "Donuts? Don't you know you should keep donuts away from an *infertile* woman?"

2) "So I'm talking to this other *infertile* about what kind of car makes sense..."

3) "Should he leave his wife at home to travel, especially when she's *infertile?*"

4) "As an *infertile* woman, I believe it's important that good healthcare insurance be available.

5) "Now that I'm *infertile*, I have so little time to read."

Now what was that about me focusing too much on my lack of fertility? Try listening a little differently to conversations the next time you're out and about. Along the same lines, I also amended part of an article I found online about the identity crisis mothers face, to offer a satirical look at life as an infertile. I'm sure you can figure out which word has been replaced.

Finding Your Personal Identity as an Infertile

When Betty asked me at a family wedding, "So what are you doing now?" I completely froze. I had no clue what to say. I had chosen, for better or worse, to be a stay-at-home infertile. Fortunately for me, Betty sensed my discomfort and chose to rephrase her question, "What would you like to be doing?" ...

After that encounter, it became clear to me that my identity had always been tied into my career. Without it, I didn't know who I was. I was an infertile, but who was I really?

While many women thrive on their infertile status and are content with it, others feel a strong need to have a personal identity beyond their roles as infertiles and struggle with the change. It's sometimes hard to remember that aside from our roles as infertiles, we are individuals with interests, passions, and desires—and we must be able to fulfill those needs to be the best infertiles—and people—possible. ...

According to my doctor, it didn't matter if an infertile wanted to work or if she wanted to stay at home full time—

the most important thing was that it had to be the infertile's choice. "Whichever path you choose make sure you take care of yourself in the process. A happy infertile makes the best infertile," she advised...

Ah yes, some parts of society routinely found a whole lot more emotional support than others. Sometimes I stored up the anger, allowing it to build like a volcano, while other times I just let it blow. Like the time I was with Alex on a weekend getaway to the California wine country. I was doing my best to mind my own bid'ness. Everything was copacetic until some fertiles, well, taunted me, and this wasn't a Momzilla, but Gramzilla.

It was 6:45 pm. My guy and I entered a fine dining wine country restaurant in late February. To our right, a large fire roared. To our left was a dining area where among other tables there was a party of eight people seated – three of whom were under the age of five. I made a mental note to seat ourselves as far away as possible when kids were prominent in a restaurant other than the likes of McDonald's, Bakers Square or Chuck E. Cheese. Just to be sure that we had some uninterrupted romantic time I selected a cozy table in the bar to enjoy a light meal with my squeeze. *Let me repeat, we were seated in the area of the restaurant where alcoholic beverages were served to people 21 years of age and older.* At a small table nearby sat another couple sharing a light meal in the bar. *Did I mention we were in a bar?* The romantic ambiance of the place was torpedoed within minutes by the table with the kidlets. It started with shrieking and fussing from the youngest, a toddler in a high chair. It was further aggravated by the toddler's table mates, two little girls in party dresses who started using their "outside voices." I was irritated but I said to myself, *I'm going to do my best to ignore them. They're over there, I'm over here.*

The waiter brought two glasses of a lovely, local red varietal wine. We perused the menu and ordered a risotto dish. The adults in the party of eight were about to finish their meals and the little ones grew more restless by the minute. I wondered how much longer the adults were going to test the kids by keeping them cooped up at the table. Clearly at 7:30 in the evening the toddler and little girls should have preferred to be home watching the Cartoon Network or Nickelodeon before bath time. The toddler let out a world-class sneeze and started coughing his brains out. I was thankful that we were outside the germ zone.

Our food arrived just as the adults at the table of eight kicked back to let their food digest. Eager to nurture their food-induced stupor, they released the two girls who – delighted to be free – scampered around the bar in what amounted to tap shoes, unsupervised. CLACK, CLACK, CLACK on the hardwood floor they went running by our table in one direction. CLACK, CLACK, CLACK. They returned to the big table to report on what they'd found. CLACK, CLACK, CLACK they were off again this time playing hide-and-go-seek amid the bar sofas. I felt my blood pressure rise. To my left the toddler appeared in my line of sight walking with as much coordination as a drunk, holding his bottle of milk. I was immediately left wondering when he was going to cough and sneeze again.

A mother (or aunt figure) realized after five minutes or more that he'd disappeared and went off in search of the lost boy. The little girls continued frolicking around our table as though they were on a playground. I saw the couple at the other table stiffen. They were clearly bothered, too.

Then I had my own Norma Rae or Howard Beale moment. I was not going to just gnash my teeth and submit. I was mad as hell and I was not going to take it anymore. I calmly pushed back my chair, walked over to one of the errant young women coming back by our table with the toddler in tow and said in an even keel but firm tone, "Excuse me, but this is NOT 'Romper Room.' This is a bar. It is not appropriate for children to be playing here."

I slipped back into my seat while the somewhat mystified woman rounded up the three children in the bar and took them back to their table. Not less than five minutes later, a positively indignant Gramzilla marched over and got in my face while I cut a piece of asparagus. She defiantly held her tired and fussy grandson whose nose desperately needed to be wiped. She was seething. In a voice loud enough for everyone seated at the bar and immediate area to hear she hissed at me, "When I called this restaurant I asked if it was okay to bring children. They told me I could. You have ... well, you need to think about where YOU are!"

I thought: *I AM IN A BAR. Why is this crazy lady holding a baby (in a bar!) confronting me. Why is she implying that I am out of line? Would Alex and I go into a Chuck E. Cheese and demand that all of the kids be quiet so we could enjoy a romantic dinner?*

I was almost speechless. Almost. Then, her chastising complete, she turned on her heel holding her grandson triumphantly. And that's when it happened.

Every meal I'd ever had interrupted by someone's overtired, loudly whining child, every romantic evening trashed because parents put their own convenience ahead of the consideration of others, and visions of every Momzilla, Dadzilla, Gramzilla who gave their children permission to have the run of non-kid places came bubbling up inside me.

"F@#$ YOU!" I said in the same tone of voice she had used on me. And then I raised my hand and flipped off the entire table of inconsiderate adults. Their inability to consider how their children might be affecting others was their way of saying f@#$ you to those of us in the bar. It just seemed the right thing to do. Interestingly, the adults managed to contain the children in their dining area while we finished our meal.

But I was still annoyed. Annoyed that I had to be put in the position of bad guy. Really, did I need to be antagonized on top of having to adjust to living in the world of the fertile? Gramzillas? Now I had to look out for Gramzillas?

It reminded me that infertility didn't end with the baby-making years. Reminders of our truncated family tree cropped up in the oddest places. There was the time I went to the hardware store to get some gardening tools. At the checkout an affable woman who would have been at the senior center if she hadn't been working the cash register asked to see my driver's license. I was a brunette, though the six-year-old picture on my license showed me as a blond. I jokingly assured her that it really was me in the photo, despite my penchant for changing hair styles and color.

My chatty cashier then launched into a monologue that began with, "Just wait until the day comes when you have grandchildren and they refuse to believe, despite evidence, you were ever young once..."

I didn't hear much of what followed next in her story. I was too busy debating whether I should let her continue to ramble or school her in the fact that not every woman is predetermined to become a grandmother. This time a kinder voice in my head won out. She hadn't intended to provoke a lesson in endocrinology. I gathered up my purchases and left the store. The rest of the day the debate continued to rage inside my head. An angry voice refused to let it go. It told me that I shouldn't have let her off the hook so easily. I should have set her straight on her misplaced assumptions. And while I did come up with zingers I could have used, it was small consolation.

Later that weekend on a hunt for books at the library about life after infertility (yeah, big selection, BIG selection, NOT!), another landmine of sorts awaited me. In the display case sat a book called *Beyond the Mommy Years*. Just seeing the cover filled me with quiet rage. A photo of a soapy knee bent in a tub and a hand holding a glass of wine implying a celebration of a job well done. A victory for having made it to a new stage of life. A voice inside my head said, "Walk away. You do not want to pick this particular book up. Keep moving!"

What did I do? Not only did I pick it up, I checked it out.

Yeah, the book sat on my kitchen counter for a week before I felt ready to crack the spine. I waited for the inevitable – a need to vent my anger. The jacket cover read: "Thirty million mothers between 40 and 60 years old are about to face childless households for the first time in decades. And for many, the community found on the playground, on the playing fields, and even at PTA meetings is gone."

Oh, reaaaaaallllly? And I'm supposed to feel BAD for these women? They're feeling grief, you say? They're trying to figure out this "postmommyhood" (the author's term) stage of their life? Boo-hoo. Well get in the BACK of the line, ladies. You've got some serious hard time to do before you're going to find any sympathy from the likes of me. Try living the empty nest syndrome of a different flavor, a barren nest, and *then* we can talk. Until then, well...you don't really want to know what I'm thinking. What other pearls of wisdom are contained in this book?

Well alllllrighty ... First and foremost, apparently I've been looking at this post-mommyhood/post-infertility treatment stage of life all wrong! How could I have been so silly!? Our *Beyond the Mommy Years* author points to postmommyhood exhibit "A," Jasmine, who explained that "It's only now after her children are gone that she has awakened from her Mother Dream, fully energized and eager to get on with the rest of her life."

Hmmm, let me see if I follow. Now that I'm no longer under the illusion that one day I'll miraculously conceive, I just need to wake up and shake off my Infertility Drea... well, in my case it was no "dream," it was a NIGHTMARE!

Yeah, see, this doesn't quite apply. I think it's a tad easier to move out of the postmommyhood *dream* state with a visit to the mall – what better time to ditch those Mom Jeans? Nightmares, on the other hand, well, they have a way of leaving in their wake a little unfinished business ... it's going to take more than a new outfit to get "energized." Now, what else does the author propose?

Savor the remaining moments.

You're kidding, right? There's very little about the years in the conception failure loop that I want to savor. Maybe the Valium that I got to take on my embryo transfer day, yeah, that was pretty good stuff, but outside of that no, not much to savor I'm afraid.

You see, while age-wise those in the mommy species will one day join me in living without children, I'm guessing there will always be a gulf between us given our defining years as "fertiles" and "infertiles." How can there not be, when the stuff of bonding is made up of reminiscing about shared moments – like what it felt like to meet your first RE team, or the first time you tried to give yourself an injection consisting of the urine of post-menopausal women, or...

What? You have no idea what RE refers to? You mean, you *didn't* shoot up Pergonal? Well, okay how about those minor nervous breakdowns when Aunt Flo arrived? You mean you *liked* it when Aunt Flo arrived?

Hmmm, again. I kind of wondered if we two different species of women would ever find a way back to each other when we stopped cycling once and for all, but I gotta say fertiles will need to do some work first, and it involves getting outside of their cozy little bubble to fully appreciate the infertile's mindset – the equivalent would be wrapping their head around the notion of *Beyond the Barren Years...*

We infertiles have already done our homework. We're painfully aware of the "fertile's lifestyle" and the related empty nest syndrome. How can we *not* be when just about every sitcom, drama and news show is made up of parenting tales? So, until there's some measure of understanding about what it means to live the barren years, I'm guessing bonding tomorrow with the postmommyhood crowd – just like today's mommy crowd – is gonna be a bit of a challenge.

Apparently if you can't have children, living in a child-centric world can really fry your tomatoes. I never imagined it would be like this. I never thought being unable to have children would so radically affect me day to day, week to week and year to year. Much as I *wanted* to forget about what had turned my life upside down, I couldn't. Trapped at a party or a work event with parents riffing about junior's latest exploits, or worse, stuck between women comparing pregnancy symptoms, I found myself wondering which was worse – listening to them or a root canal without Novocaine. Most days I'd have taken the latter. The physical pain was far easier to manage. Then I'd fantasize about getting a wine IV to dull the pain. I didn't care if I would have to pay for it with a colossal hangover later. Is it any wonder that segregation had a mighty strong appeal?

So how was I faring in my post-apocalyptic infertile hell? Well, let's see. Now approaching my forty-third birthday, I was having more good days in my life, but in my angriest moments I was still unable to see that not all mothers and fathers were alike. There was a time I believed that we would forever live in separate camps, incapable of ever finding common ground. Too often the few fertiles who expended any energy thinking about their infertile sisterhood or brotherhood devolved into talking smack about crazed infertiles and the lengths they go to start their families. Infertiles, meanwhile, railed about the ignorance of fertiles. Sigh. Just not pretty. And who benefited? No one. Not a soul.

CHAPTER SIX

A SILVER BULLET?
NOT SO FAST, COWBOY

*L*et's see a show of hands. How many of you are dying to ask: "Pam, have you thought about adoption?"

We not only *thought* about it. We looked into it.

Since I was forty years old and Alex was forty-five when we pulled the plug on fertility treatments, we faced a sizeable, protracted uphill battle to become parents through adoption, and like IVF, without any guarantees of success. The system favored those younger than forty years old. Furthermore, since single motherhood had shed its stigma (the controversy years earlier around Murphy Brown notwithstanding) fewer babies – no longer considered "illegitimate" – were put up for adoption. By 1980, less than three percent of non-married women under twenty-five years of age chose adoption for their child. Over ninety percent of private adoptions today are open, where birthparents choose the adoptive parents and some exchange identifying information. We'd been told by friends and acquaintances who had adopted to expect that we'd be forming a relationship with more than a child – we'd be also be forming a relationship with the child's extended family. And while it's the exception rather than the rule for birth parents to lay claim to their offspring after agreements or contracts are in place, the potential exists. I was more than a little affected by the national news-making "Baby M" case in the days when I was still convinced I was a Fertile Myrtle. The story involved

a surrogate mother, who was also the biological mother, initiating a protracted and ugly legal fight with the biological father and his wife over
custody of Baby M. It made a deep and lasting impression on me. The
images of a scared and crying toddler at the heart of the case tugged at
my heart. Not long after that event, by strange coincidence, a work colleague also lost an infant a month after the birth mother changed her
mind about relinquishing her parental rights. Worse still, the same thing
happened a second time they tried to adopt.

Around the time we were winding down fertility treatment we made
a few field trips to learn more about the various adoption options. We
were fortunate to have friends and colleagues generous with their time
and insights as well as their honesty. One colleague, "Burt," when an-
nouncing the adoption of his third child, invited and answered any and
all questions about his experience – even volunteering that each of his
children had different birth mothers.

There's nothing like the topic of reproduction and birth-mother talk
to collapse the personal boundaries that normally exist in an office setting. Burt and I quickly got down to brass tacks. He and his wife had
looked into IVF. They'd even met with the same doctors we had six years
earlier. Given their ages at the time, almost forty, and the doctors' less
than encouraging diagnosis, they had decided they didn't want to waste
time playing the expensive game of assisted reproductive roulette. They
focused their attention and finances instead on private placement adoption. Burt suggested we learn more about his blended family by joining
them for dinner. We settled on a Friday night.

The sound of kids playing greeted us as we exited our car. Burt's
cozy stucco house had an enclosed front courtyard that offered an area
where children could safely use their outside voices and run about while
still under the supervision of a parent working in the kitchen with one or
both eyes trained on a picture window.

We came upon what appeared to be a five-year-old and a three-year-
old playing a game of hot potato. The younger of the two stopped her

activity and ran up to inspect us. She held up three fingers and declared, "I'm 'Jenny' and I'm free!"

Burt scooped up his nearly five-year-old son like a battering ram and walked over to greet us. He swung his son "Adam" to the ground to free his arms, gave me a hug and shook hands with Alex.

"Welcome to Chez Chaos. 'Diane' is inside changing 'Eric's' diaper. Let's find her."

There was a half-wall separating the tiled foyer from the kitchen area. A bulletin board next to the phone was full of crayoned and penciled drawings, liberally decorated with sparkles. Underneath the board was a set of coat hooks hung lower than would be needed for an adult. On the ground was a shoe tray with a variety of flip-flops, kitten heels with soft fuzzy trim, and mini running shoes. Next to it was a step that would allow a toddler to reach up and grab a small pink fleece off of a hook.

Down the hall came Diane carrying five-month-old Eric. She placed her wrapped bundle into my arms and said, "I hate to put you to work before we've had a chance to meet properly but I've got a sauce that needs stirring on the stove."

I was struck by how solid Eric was. He weighed significantly more than I expected. I looked down at his chubby cheeks and dark eyes. He didn't fuss or seem the least bit perturbed that he was in the arms of a stranger. I realized how awkward it felt to hold a baby. I'd avoided baby-passing exercises ever since it had become evident that pregnancy might not come easily. Jenny, meanwhile, took Alex's hand and tugged him toward the family room.

"Want to see my dollhouse?" she asked without waiting for an answer.

"It sure looks like you two are ready to be parents," Burt said emphatically as he headed into the kitchen to help set the table. "Just make sure you start the college fund immediately. It's gonna cost you dearly to pay tuition in 2018!

"Hey, can I get you something to drink? A juice box? Some Kool-aid? Or we have adult beverages. Beer or wine?"

A few minutes later Jenny and Adam were engrossed in a video of *Beauty and the Beast* on the television set around the corner. Eric was resting comfortably in a baby seat decorated by a collection of shapes that arced over his head within reach, should he have chosen to explore further. Alex and I sat nervously next to each other on a sofa. In the car ride over we had both expressed discomfort about how many questions we should ask. And then with the kids within earshot we weren't sure where the lines should be drawn or how to discuss the subject. Diane and Burt arrived from the kitchen, each carrying a glass of wine for us.

Burt cut to the chase. "So, you're looking into adoption? That's great! We're clearly all for it."

Looking over at Diane with a loving smile he added, "We couldn't be happier with our brood, could we, honey?"

Diane returned the smile. "Sleep deprivation aside, Eric makes up for it by being a cuddle-monster."

"Well," Burt said. "We're happy to share our experience. There are no off-limit questions in this house. Feel free to ask whatever comes to mind.

"Oh, and by the way," he added. "The kids know all about their adoption. They've seen pictures of their birth mothers and we get regular cards and gifts from at least one of their biological grandmas."

I couldn't hide my astonishment.

"We decided it was worth it to have an open adoption, and some of the hairiness associated with it, to save time and start our family sooner," he added.

Diane explained further. "We have friends who pursued the closed adoption route with a number of domestic and international adoption agencies. They had to wait nearly ten years to adopt a baby. It's competitive to get a healthy baby if you're Caucasian or want the child to resemble you in any way. It's even more impossible if one of you is forty years old, which we both were when we started. There's no extra credit for wisdom, financial security or life experience. The 'system' prefers parents under forty."

Burt reached for a cracker and cheese. "Just our bad luck we met when we were thirty-eight and married at thirty-nine. The time crunch was on big time! By the way, since the late '90s almost all adoptions have been 'open.' That means that if they decide they – the biological parents and kids who know they've been adopted – want to find each other in the future, they will not be restricted like in the old days."

He paused for a moment, chewing, and then shrugged his shoulders. "You just have to get used to the fact that you're raising someone else's kids."

He disappeared for a moment and returned with what looked like a laminated report and a flyer. He placed them on the coffee table in front of us. "The first thing we did after accumulating as much as we could in our savings account – hey, you think IVF is expensive, adoption costs will trump that any day of the week – was find a great attorney who specializes in private placement adoption. She told us that the best way to increase our chances of success would be to cast the widest net we could – in other words, tell everyone we know, and even those we don't know, that we wanted to adopt.

"You know marketing, right?" Burt asked.

I nodded and reached for my glass of wine hoping it would settle my nerves a bit.

"Well, a big part of succeeding in adoption is effectively selling you as prospective parents."

Alex moved to inspect the laminated dossier sitting on the table. On the cover was a friendly, smiling picture of Diane and Burt in a casual embrace. The copy described a loving, well-educated and financially stable couple who wanted to become parents. They shared their backgrounds, personality traits, their parenting philosophy and their qualifications for raising children. Also inside were endorsements from friends, clergy, and bosses along with more pictures of them doing what they love most – biking, hiking and camping.

The one-page flyer next to the brochure was less revealing but still to the point. A headline over a photo of the two of them read, "We'd Like to Adopt." The copy advised the reader to consider contacting them through their attorney if they knew of any pregnant women who were considering giving up their babies for adoption.

Diane reached over to rock Eric in his infant seat. "We posted the flyers in churches, mailed them to high school counselors' offices and shared them with colleagues at work. It took about a year before we heard from our attorney that the single mother of a high school junior had interest in meeting us. She and her pregnant daughter both agreed she was too young to parent a child. That's ultimately how we got Adam."

"Basically you have to find a pregnant teenage girl," Burt added matter of factly. "That's where the market is. Their loss is your gain. This is not the Brady Bunch, mind you, it's never that clean."

Beauty and the Beast had lost its hold on Jenny and Adam. They practically tripped each other running back into the room looking for dinner. "We're hungry, Mom," they said in unison as they clamored onto the sofa and found room on either side of Diane for a snuggle.

After dinner I joined Diane in the kitchen to scoop some ice cream while the guys talked sports in the other room. That's when she dropped her voice to a whisper and said, "Listen, there's one other thing I need to tell you, and this isn't easy to say…but you need to know that adoption doesn't erase the desire I still feel to have my own biological kids."

I was surprised to hear this admission, given how genuinely affectionate Diane was with her children.

"Don't get me wrong. I love Adam, Jenny and Eric to bits. I would do anything for them. They are my family, my priority, but there remains a longing still to know what sort of child Burt and I might have created."

Diane suddenly looked guilty about her confession and moved to end the conversation. "This ice cream is melting fast. Let's get it out to the guys before it becomes soup. Then I have to double check Eric's diaper. He's like clockwork after his feeding."

On the drive home Alex and I wondered aloud what it would be like in ten or fifteen years when Burt and Diane's kids were older and wanted to know even more about the circumstances of their adoption and their biological family trees. It seemed only natural, especially in the confusing teenage years, for kids to want to know more about their identities, where they came from.

In the end, we had no interest in "selling ourselves" to a birth mother, of getting into a new and long line of couples waiting and wondering if we might one day be selected. I was done with waiting and wondering. My heart couldn't risk the idea of being broken again. Weary and wary, we made the decision to be the best aunt and uncle we knew how to be to our immediate families' and friends' children. But, for the record, I've since learned from some of my infertile sisters who did move ahead with adoption that scars remained. Once infertile, always infertile. Much as we gals might want to disregard how infertility changed us, it wasn't something that could be pretended away. I wasn't alone in my thinking. Here, a few thoughts shared with me by infertile women who went on to adopt:

"Adoption is not some panacea for infertility. It is a decision that requires a lot of thought and care, and saying that someone should adopt so they'll get pregnant is a total slap in the face to any adopted child. Anyway, I would like to tell fertiles that even though I'm a mom, I'm still infertile. I've experienced the same loss as women who chose not to parent [as a result of infertility]. In addition, I'm going to have to deal with all those same losses when my daughter conceives. I'm going to have to deal with the additional loss of three children who have lost their birth families, their heritage, their self-identity, their first mother."

"Even though my children are in your class I'm not the same mom as you. I'm still scarred, hormonal, mourning, and hurt. I'm still an infertile woman and will be for the rest of my life. I never left the infertility bandwagon however resolved my 'need' to have children via adoption is. My oldest is now sixteen. I still HATE baby showers, LOVE that having a baby hurts so badly and that post-baby bodies are not as toned. Bitter that I couldn't have my own? Yes! In love with my two children, more than you can know. I'm living with post-infertility trauma, even now fighting depression, anger, and physical pain."

"I am a step-mother, and I'd like birth mothers to know that YES

I STILL MOTHER CHILDREN, even though I didn't give birth to them! People constantly talk to my husband about 'his' kids and totally ignore me in conversations. We were contemplating adopting a child, and I realized that it still wouldn't matter – people would still look at me and say I had no 'real' children. (Not that having society accept me is a good reason to adopt. I'm just saying.) While my husband understands why this situation infuriates me, he can't really fully appreciate why it saddens and angers me. I accepted his children when I accepted his offer of marriage, thinking I could love them as my own. And I can and do. No one else seems to see that though."

So, in the interest of making the world a better place for my fellow infertiles (and to be certain that I'm heard I'm going to turn up the volume here): DON'T _EVER_ ASK AN INFERTILE PERSON IF THEY HAVE CONSIDERED ADOPTION. There are few more insulting, dismissive and downright ignorant questions you can ask.

OF COURSE WE'VE CONSIDERED ADOPTION!

Why is the question insulting? Because there's nothing wrong with our _brains_, it's our _reproductive organs_ that are messed up. When one finds out that one can't have children the old-fashioned way one looks at _all_ available options. One of them is, DUH, adoption. You're not telling us anything we don't already know. A wealth of books, articles and websites provide chapter and verse on the ins and outs of open and closed adoption, domestic and international adoption, foster care adoption and embryo adoption. (I bet you didn't even know about that last one!) The question also implies that children are as interchangeable as Swatch watches or iPod skins. THEY ARE HUMAN BEINGS, not accessories.

Why is the question dismissive? Because asking the question implies that there was no loss, sorrow, disappointment, shock, longing, grief, heartache or dashed dreams associated with not being able to bear children. Would you be so uncaring as to ask a parent who has buried a child if they've contacted the local foster care system yet to get a replacement child for the one they lost? Sounds a tad insensitive maybe?

And, lastly, it's ignorant because it implies that adoption agencies operate like some sort of call center – "operators are standing by to take your order" for a child.

Now how prepared would you be in the wake of the emotional, physical and financial stress I've just shared to flip a switch and:

1. Allow what amounts to inspectors (social workers) into your house for home study evaluations that include various background checks?

2. Answer wide-ranging questions about your sex life? Your emotional state? Your finances? Your health? Your parenting style? Your religious beliefs?

3. Get letters of recommendation from friends, family members, and colleagues that explain how and why you are "fit" to parent?

4. Write a letter to a birth mother making a case for why she should turn over her baby to you?

5. Pay thousands of dollars (the average domestic adoption runs $15,000 to $30,000 and international adoptions closer to $50,000 or more), and fill out mountains of paperwork?

6. Wait an average of two years (though this can take much longer in closed or international adoptions)?

7. Live with the knowledge that one day you might hear "but you're not my *real* mom or dad – I'd really like to find them."

It doesn't end there. Then the prospective parent's age, sexual orientation, marriage and, more recently, body mass index (BMI) and weight come into play.

Now what was that you were saying about *just* adopting? And, furthermore, if adoption is the "right" thing to do why isn't it suggested to couples *before* they try to start a family under their own steam? Once, after listening to a mother of three extol the virtues of adoption and giving a child a home I asked her why she didn't adopt. "Well, I have my own," she incredulously replied.

Ah yes, in our lighter moments we who can't have children fantasize about watching such cavalier question-posing types go through the above hoops and more to demonstrate *their* fitness to be a parent.

CHAPTER SEVEN

DEPRESSION: IT'S SOUL DEADENING TO BE INFERTILE, NEXT QUESTION?

Ugh. Just looking at this chapter heading makes me, well, depressed. I'll try to keep this one fairly short. My depression wasn't even all that out of the ordinary or impressive, but what it lacked in drama it made up for in length. A low-grade depression started not long after I stopped hanging out in doctor offices. After a brief but volatile angry phase, depression returned with a vengeance. When not at work with my door closed trying to avoid all but necessary contact, I spent most of that phase of my life asleep. Sleep could be great when it was restful, but I had a series of really bad dreams throughout that awful period. I wasn't safe from the infertility monster, even in the far-off reaches of deep slumber.

I found myself routinely awakened by awful dreams that had a common theme – people mocking or shunning me for my childlessness. In one unsettling dream around Christmas-time (one of the worst holidays, second only to Mother's Day in my opinion), I approached a shopping mall door only to have a security guard bar my entrance, demanding evidence of children before he'd let me in. Peering inside I saw parents and their children lined up to visit with Santa. There before me was a magical world of lights and music and laughter, which I was not permitted to enter. In another pajama fit, I repeatedly opened my mailbox to find it empty while my neighbors pulled from their mailboxes stacks of greeting and photo cards with beaming families in their holiday finery down to the littlest ones with faux reindeer headbands or elf shoes. These nightmarish episodes followed by insomnia were becoming far too familiar. When conscious, my depression alternated with residual anger. They played hide and seek like old pals. They really were two sides of the same coin.

So there was the *delusion* of being "done" with the whole trying to conceive/infertility thing and the *reality* of being "done." As I crept closer to my mid-forties and realized that I was quickly closing in on the end of my eggs ever pulling out the stops or heaving a final Hail Mary pass, I began what became a two year dance with grief. Infertility had moved from a predominantly physical battle to a mental one. Melancholy finally overtook anger.

A flyer on the porch promoted a Goodwill drive. Good thing, because I was feeling the need to purge. I grabbed two boxes from the garage and worked my way from the kitchen back to the bedrooms tossing in everything from extra utensils to old towels to barely used, once fashionable purses. Then I came upon the closet with the cardboard box marked "BABY." As I pulled it down from the shelf a little yellow onesie arm flopped open as if to offer a hug. I crumpled in a heap and started to convulse in tears. After nearly half an hour of sobbing, I reached over to collect the balls of soggy snot-filled tissues and deposit them in a trash can. With eerie calm I made my way to the bathroom sink and bathed my hot and swollen face with cool water. I knew that it was time to donate the box of baby outfits I'd accumulated over the years. I filled another bag with anything resembling maternity wear. I was convinced that I'd somehow managed to curse our efforts by prematurely bringing these items into the house anyway. Crazy, sure, but when overcome with grief, thoughts were far from logical.

Maybe it was time for some shock therapy? Like how about hearing the word MOM used fifty times in less than an hour? It's a little word, but it packs a punch: MOM. There I was in a business presentation on the power and reach of today's growing and influential "Mom's Clubs."

As the presenter made her case, the word came at me with increasing force: mom, Mom, MOM!!

I could literally feel myself twitching as if getting an electric shock each time the speaker uttered it, placing the emphasis on the MOM of Mom's Clubs. On the screen behind her were adorable images of children hugging their moms, moms looking concerned while tending to a child or moms laughing with other moms, exchanging knowing glances because they shared the trust and loyalty of their MOM's Club. By the end of the presentation I was convinced that my life would forever be lacking in camaraderie, joy and togetherness. As a non-mom, I'd never get the little jokes, the inside community scoop, the invitations to hang out in the MOM's Club and the benefit of having an ever-expanding community social calendar knit together with children's play dates or cupcake recipe swapping. You see, MOMs are more organized than ever today. I learned there are nearly 5,000 MOM's Clubs in the U.S. with an average of 200 members (working and stay-at-home moms alike) all busy swapping ideas, creating events and networking with other moms, usually under the leadership of what was no doubt a Queen Bee MOM.

Sigh. There was a day when I associated the word mom with warmth, goodness, band-aids lovingly applied, and cookies. The way it got tossed around now it conferred some type of elevated status. When I was a child my mother hung out with neighborhood women while the kids ran around the local park, Scout troop outing or ice cream social with, let's face it, nowhere near today's helicopter parental supervision. My mother and those in her peer group were nothing like twenty-first century MOMs who seem to take being a MOM to a new extreme. And because of to-day's newfound pride (I am MOM hear me roar, I belong to a MOM's CLUB!), they've left non-Moms feeling unwelcome and dare I say it, unworthy, because we're not, yes, MOMs. No child. Sorry, no admission to the Club. Funny thing, my mother always told me to make sure to have enough cupcakes for everyone and not to make others feel left out.

While we're on the MOM subject, I'd like to talk about Mother's Day for a minute. There is no more dreaded time of the year for infertiles.

Short of locating an atomic bomb shelter to hang out in for the first ten or fifteen days of May, there's no way to avoid the bombardment of online, TV and prints ads or the point-of-purchase displays everywhere celebrating that which some of us can't achieve. You have no idea how many times I've had customer service people randomly wish me a "Happy Mother's Day." Ouch. For more than a few years what seemed like innocuous, mistaken greeting launched me into lunar orbit. *Seriously? How about Happy Halloween?'Cause that's really how this holiday feels to me - macabre.* It did seem odd that any woman who pushed out a baby instantly got elevated to sainthood. Did they hand out halos in the labor and delivery room? (My personal candidate for sainthood was Alex. There should be statues erected in his honor, songs sung about him. He had been far and away the most patient, loving, giving person on the planet.)

Maybe it was the self-importance, the false modesty of Mother's Day that drove me mad. It just seemed unfair somehow. I've known plenty of women who were single or childfree by choice who were incredibly nurturing, giving people. I've also known women who delivered one or more children who were more concerned with themselves than their little ones. The attention and adulation, it seemed, would be better focused on women who truly earned the right to be held up as model Madonnas (not the rocker type, but the real deal).

While I made a fuss over my own my mother, I avoided the pageantry that once had me mesmerized in the pew. Thumbing through the newspaper one weekend after the Hallmark-ized holiday, I was tickled to death to stumble across a particularly meaningful "Dear Abby" column. A reader, a "proud husband and father in the Midwest," was upset with his wife because at their church Mother's Day service:

"She refused to stand and be recognized by our community. She says she won't do it because there are women in our church who are not standing, and some of them might not be able to be mothers and may be hurt at the recognition that others are receiving." He felt that "since infertile women lived with their great loss every day he doubted that the church's annual recognition of mothers would add more pain than those women already endured."

Those women? I could feel the anger rising from my toes. It's one thing for me to think of myself as another species of woman, but this cretin wasn't fit to wipe my boots. What planet was this guy from and how did I send him back there? He then asked for Abby's support on his position. Abby, bless her soul, wrote in response:

"No, I do not agree. Your wife is a woman with unusual sensitivity and empathy for the feelings of others. I respect her stance on remaining seated, and so should you."

So, just when I thought there was no hope getting those in the fertile community to appreciate the magnitude of an infertile's ache, this gentle soul in the Midwest demonstrated a simple but profound act of defiance in support of her pregnancy-challenged sisters. I wished I knew where she lived so I could send her a bouquet of flowers.

Meanwhile, I was past due in scheduling a visit with my once-designated pregnancy pal and former cruise ship comrade. She now had three kids younger than five years of age. It had been months since we'd visited. I could have simply picked up the phone, but there remained a part of me that didn't really want to have an honest conversation about why we seemed to be drifting further and further apart. We were moving down completely different paths. Our last visit had been tense.

Her four-week-old had had a restless night, setting in motion a sequence of events that resulted in her much later-than-expected arrival for lunch. We requested a table in a less heavily trafficked back room since she planned to nurse her daughter throughout our visit. The baby was contentedly sound asleep in her carrier and seemed prepared to let her mother eat some portion of her lunch before demanding her own.

Once settled, my friend launched into a litany of how much she missed her time alone, her lack of freedom to pursue her interests and the drudgery of her daily household, homemaker routine.

I had a flashback to the early 1970s, sitting on the steps of my parents' house as I had some thirty years earlier during the "rap session" hosted by my mother. I listened as sympathetically as I could, all the while stealing glances at the sweet-faced baby who was starting to stir. Although some time had passed since starting to reconcile my infertility, I marveled nonetheless at how easily my friend had put my infertility firmly in the past. It had been nearly three years since I had stored hormones in her refrigerator during an over-night stay, but I hadn't kept it a secret that the emotional aspects of infertility were as hard as or harder to manage than the physical. Was she really openly *complaining* to me about motherhood?

Calmly slicing the fruit on her plate, she segued to the difficulties associated with getting her children into acceptable preschools. The politics, financial contributions and influence brokering necessary to gain entrance to the most sought after schools were, apparently, mind-boggling. Then with her fork poised to spear a cantaloupe slice, she stopped midsentence and radically changed gears.

"Oh, this can't be interesting to you. I'm just so used to comparing notes with moms from the playgroups. Guess I went on autopilot. I hope you don't mind. I'm just so worried about getting my kids on the best academic path. It is *always* top of mind. You know, it's become so ridiculously competitive at all levels. Whatever happened to kids having unstructured time? We managed to turn out all right. Geez, outside of Girl Scouts, I was pretty much a free to do whatever I wanted."

I told her Alex described our childhood as a bygone one of "free range kids."

She paused to consider that idea and then found a new train of thought. Her face lit up. "You know, you'd really like my friends Rene and Maureen. Rene is a former marketing executive and Maureen, well, she had to undergo some eight IVF treatments before finally delivering Kingston." (*Or was it Dakota or Bismarck? What was the deal with these goofy names parents were laying on their kids?*) I think you'd enjoy them. They're not your typical suburban super-moms. Would you be interested?"

I grimaced. I could feel my face flushing in anger.

"To be honest, I've got more acquaintances and friends in the 'mom friend' category than I can handle. At this point, I'm more interested in meeting and befriending women who don't have kids, either by choice or some fluke of nature. Not to sound too discriminatory, I'd also be open to women who have grown kids and are beyond the potty-training, 'time out' stage of their lives."

Seeing my friend recoil, I tried to soften my objections.

"You have to understand. I'm not going to lie about it. Your transition to motherhood has been really hard for me. And to be brutally honest, I have no interest in seeking to expand a circle of friends whose predominant identity or occupation centers around the care and feeding of kids – especially those who are not yet self-sufficient."

Her face fell and her shoulders hunched forward as though cumulative weariness was taking hold. The baby began a staccato cry signaling her hunger. Scooping the little one up and tossing a blanket over her left shoulder, my friend maneuvered her daughter under cover and onto her breast, flashing the table behind us briefly in the process.

"Really, I had no idea my life turned you off so much. I know your experience has made coping with the whole motherhood thing difficult, but you really seemed like you've moved on in the last year."

Effortlessly switching her daughter from her left to right breast, she continued.

"Does this mean you don't want anything to do with my kids? Are you telling me that I have to edit out large chunks of my life from now on when we talk?"

Looking for a way to make things work between us, I forged ahead with a suggestion.

"Let's try to pattern-match our conversations a bit. I'll avoid mentions about how I spent a lazy summer afternoon – whether in the backyard sipping a gin and tonic while thumbing through my favorite fashion magazine or on a mindless shoe-shopping expedition. Why torture you?"

By the same token I suggested she direct her conversations about the joy of first words or triumphant potty training with women who could best relate to those experiences. She wasn't entirely willing to sign up to that strategy.

"But I want to know there's freedom out there. I want to live vicariously through your shoe scavenger hunts, and God, I'd kill for a nap."

Fortunately the bill arrived. What I didn't say was, *yeah, but I don't want to be reminded of the significant parts of my life that won't be happening. The hole in my heart feels large enough already.*

For an extended period we continued to drift further and further apart. Phone calls became less regular. The urgency to schedule visits evaporated. The mental distance brought on a different form of loss. Where my friends and I once had the ability to read each other's minds and finish each other's sentences, my child-centric friends shared more in common now with … well, my mother … than with me. The truth was, I just didn't know how to relate to them anymore, and they didn't know how to relate to me. Alex and I had grown accustomed to broken plans or being put on the bench because the needs of our family and friends' kids, naturally, came first.

The birth of my friend's third child had been a shock to my system. That's because we had finally reached a point, after baby number two was toddling along, where we could find a few hours each month to reconnect just us two old friends – no kids, no interruptions. She was no longer sleep-deprived and with her life back under control she eagerly arranged to meet me for tea, lunch or a pedicure. We would talk about politics, books, you name it. I had my old friend back.

Enter the adorable newborn. I had convinced myself during her latest pregnancy that the wounds from my unsuccessful attempts had healed. Seeing my friend nurse during lunch was both beautiful and hard to bear. I was not yet ready to be so close to the newborn experience. Much as I wanted to convince myself otherwise, a wave of emotions washed over me and pulled me under. It was just too powerful to observe the mother/nursing newborn bond – too overwhelming and sad for someone who knew she wouldn't ever experience it firsthand. Back to square one. Damn. I thought I was getting better.

Time to hit the library to see if I could locate some middle-age crisis books, or some such self-helpie thing to help me understand my malaise. I also had an addiction to books that amounted to social commentary about infertility – *The Baby Business*, *Everything Conceivable*, and similar titles – most of which condemned the industry and insinuated that people who used the services were a tad wacko (*bear in mind the old adage that I can criticize my family but you can't*). Perhaps most curiously of all: the vast majority of infertility books had been written by mothers. Not exactly the archetype an infertile woman can relate to. Most mother-authors wrote what amounted to "This, too, can happen for you" memoirs. Some even flipped to the dark side and became Momzillas, convinced their path to success was the righteous one. What is it they say? Converts make the worst zealots?

Back home with a stack of books in hand I settled onto my sofa. I came across a passage that stopped me cold. I felt a sob build deep inside. Tears, it seemed, were never far from the surface, but even I was taken by surprise at my visceral and immediate response. This time they were tears of relief. For being accepted, not judged. For being acknowledged not marginalized. For being seen as human and not as some sort of freak. Here's the passage that caused the waterworks:

"Recently married, Reverend Beth, who was in her early thirties, was looking forward to starting a family of her own. She felt acute empathy for anybody who wanted children and could not have them easily....she had already counseled a surprising number: not just women but men, and not just people who were actively trying but older couples who had confided to her their permanent sense of loss at never having had the child they longed for. [She] knew that suffering is part of human existence...Infertility had always seemed to her an especially hard form of suffering to inflict."

What stunned me upon reflection was how starved I was for such heartfelt empathy from society. Here I was a few years post-treatment, grateful for the kind thoughts of a stranger. I didn't know Reverend Beth, but like the woman in the Midwest who refused to stand at her church's Mother's Day ceremony, I was grateful to learn these lovely people existed.

Music was another way to help me escape my sadness. In 2005, while I was bouncing between anger and depression we visited my parents in Michigan. They had season tickets for the Detroit Symphony Orchestra and took us to a concert. Murmurings and laughter filled the hall as chimes signaled that the concert was about to begin. It was a treat to hear an orchestra perform live. I had taken piano lessons as a girl from a woman who played from time to time with the Windsor symphony. I enjoyed losing myself in the music. The sound of the violins could make the hair on the back of my neck stand up. Strings in particular had such a haunting quality. I envied those who made such moving, beautiful music.

I followed Alex and my parents up steep stairs into the balcony to row N and over a few feet into the seat matching my ticket. The orchestra members down below were tuning their instruments. A happy cacophony filled the auditorium. In a matter of seconds the noisy background grew silent as a female guest conductor strode across the stage. The audience came alive with applause. She took a quick bow and reached over for a wireless microphone.

In a deep and pleasing voice she brought the audience into an intimate understanding of the piece we were about to hear, "Concierto de Aranjuez." The composer, Spanish classical guitarist Joaquín Rodrigo, had been born in Valencia, Spain in 1901 on November twenty-second, which was also the birthday of Saint Cecilia, the patron saint of music. At the age of three, Rodrigo was completely blinded due to diphtheria. Amid all of the challenges he faced in his life, there was a particularly painful episode that was the inspiration for the second movement of the next piece, the Adagio – the death of his first child. I leaned forward in rapt attention. In the seat next to me a woman absentmindedly flipped through her program, as though bored by the commentary. She looked up only to glare at her young son who kept fidgeting next to her.

"This was a man," the conductor continued in a hushed voice, "who had looked forward with much joy to the birth of his first child. Tragically this baby was in this life only a very brief time. The infant passed away on the same day he was born, leaving his father devastated. The joy that had been his was turned into deep unimaginable sadness. He had had great plans for this child. He wanted to introduce him to the music and lyrics that had brought such richness to his world. What should have been one of the happiest days of his life turned out to be the saddest, as he prepared to bury his first-born. It brought him lower than he had ever thought possible.

"His world," the conductor whispered, "would never be the same. Not long after his child's death he channeled his extreme grief into this piece. In the first movement, you'll hear the joyfulness he felt in learning that he was to become a father. It's followed by the haunting sounds of the French horn signaling the loss of his beautiful baby and the life that had been taken from him. The final movement will convey the tranquility he imagined as his baby's soul made its way to heaven. You'll hear what sounds like angels greeting his precious baby as he makes his way into a place he would only know when his time came to join him."

I sat transfixed and wondered how many of the people in the festive auditorium could begin to understand the composer's grief. I inhaled sharply and held my breath, then released it slowly. The music began. With tears burning in my eyes, I blinked rapidly to stop them from rolling down my cheeks. Alex, who was watching me out of the corner of his eye, grabbed my hand tightly. The warmth of his palm reminded me that I was not alone in feeling such emotional intensity.

Minutes later a French horn began its mournful lament. I could control myself no further and leaned forward swallowing a sob that was building deep inside my chest. Taking two quick breaths I allowed the tears to quietly roll down my cheeks as the music carried me to another place. I felt an intense connection to this Spanish composer and rocked gently back and forth in my seat as the music lightened. I could feel my womb ache and throb as my period started. Even as the bleeding sensation made itself known, the heavenly music brought me closer to the sweet souls we tried to create. It was as if their spirits were in the room with us. That's when my grieving began in earnest.

Months later, my emotional gymnastics were compounded by the devastating news that my Irish sister-in-law had been diagnosed with an advanced form of lung cancer. The doctors could offer no explanation for the cause and the rapid spread. She fought valiantly with all available treatments for a brief time but the cancer was virulent and deadly. She left behind in Dublin a grief-stricken husband, a nearly ten-year-old son and a seven-year-old daughter. When Alex and I arrived at their house from the airport I did my best to try to keep it together. I wanted to do anything and everything to let my niece and nephew know that they were far from alone. We and many others would be there to help them through their nightmare. At the funeral home my niece Isabel held my hand tightly. When Isabel and I disappeared for a few minutes into the ladies room she caught me wiping my eyes and asked if I was sad. I nodded yes and stooped down to her level to give her a hug. She whispered in my ear, "When I'm sad, I try to think about other things to make me feel better." Little Izzy stunned me. I had flown more than 4,000 miles to comfort her and there she was comforting me.

A few months after the funeral she and her brother and father came to California to spend five weeks with us over their summer break. When we asked Izzy if she liked flying fourteen hours to visit us, she said with gusto, "Yes! You get to sleep whenever you want. They feed you food, and it's an adventure!"

Their visit was a big adjustment for all involved. It was the first time we'd had that much time with children under our small roof. I came away with a new appreciation for the patience required of parents. I was at the office one day when my spunky niece was coloring at the table with her uncle. Izzy stopped what she was doing to ask Alex a question. "Why don't you and Auntie Pam have any kids?"

Without missing a beat, my dear husband responded, "Well, we tried but we couldn't."

Izzy puzzled over the response for a minute, started coloring again and said, "Well, that's okay, because we all have each other."

Again. My niece cut to the chase and sized up the situation in the best way she knew how. We often say that Izzy was born without a rearview mirror. She only sees and experiences life as it unfolds in front of her. It was at times like that I realized how much I still had to learn. How proud her mother and grandmother Shirley would have been of her and her strong, optimistic orientation. Such a pity we lived so damned far apart.

Izzy wasn't the only clear-sighted female in my life. In yet another odd twist of fate, those who nurtured and cared for my battered heart with persistent gentleness were women who had never been bitten by the mother bug. While these women didn't fully comprehend my intense longing to conceive, they showered me with compassion nonetheless. They had an unusual capacity to imagine what it must feel like to want something so fundamental but always have it out of reach. When I described colleagues who squealed with delight and carried on in makeshift baby-shower behavior in the office, they groaned in disgust or jokingly offered to do harm to the offenders on my behalf. When they weren't offering their shoulders to cry on they were human signposts of a sort – providing ample evidence that women without children were still bona fide women and well-adjusted, happy ones at that. They became my "peeps."

Who were these women? Well, Susan had been my boss during one of my Silicon Valley forays. Our friendship flowered after the dot-com bust took her to Arizona. She was in a committed relationship with a younger man, never having relied on conventional roles to define her. She was the type of woman who would have thrown her belongings into a Conestoga wagon and gone west just to spite those who said she couldn't do it on her own. Tough on the outside, her voice turned soft whenever I called to get a sanity check. She marveled at the chronic carelessness others displayed. Gathering for reunions with friends who had once watched me swell with hormone shots, she would meet my gaze with exasperation when these same women pulled out photos of their children or grandchildren, completely blind to my lasting ache.

She wasn't my only "big sister." Catherine was another strong and unflappable chick – a woman who had just turned fifty and lived a life of culture and style on the Upper East Side of Manhattan. She had traveled extensively for work and pleasure over the years but had also had more than her share of heartache, losing a fiancé ten years earlier in a tragic accident. Catherine had worked with Alex before we became friends. She proved that when life served up excruciatingly hard times, one couldn't simply drown in self-pity. She demonstrated with grace and fortitude that it was possible to move forward after a body blow, to deal with periods of wishful thinking and longing the best she could without allowing it to consume her. I often wished I had even one ounce of her strength. In time I got to know Catherine well enough to divulge my futile infertility treatments. While she had never married nor had children, she showed remarkable empathy when hearing the gory details of my story.

"God, I had no idea," she said with more than a little awe. "I knew fertility clinics existed, but based on their advertising and the stories in the news, they leave you thinking they deliver – every time."

"Hardly."

"Oh, man, I just remembered Alex's face. It must have been right after the last IVF."

She teared up as she recalled the day.

"Oh, Pam. I'd never seen him that way. He's always so calm and so, well, Alex, but not that day. When I asked him what was wrong, he told me you were having a hard time with fertility stuff."

Hot tears formed as I listened.

"He said seeing you in such pain scared him. He couldn't stand to see you so sad. It was just tearing him apart. It broke my heart to see him that way."

In time I realized how much of his own suffering Alex had hidden from me. He had always done such a masterful job being strong for me. My poor, dear, sweet Alex. My own agony had forced him to do his grieving at work or silently and out of my sight.

One of the hardest things about being infertile was coming to terms or reconciling how we related to other people's children. Alex, bit by bit, acknowledged to me his discomfort when people assumed he had children just because he seemed so at ease with them. He wondered if he was being misleading by not being more upfront about our situation.

"I bet there are quite a few of my acquaintances who have no idea I'm not a dad."

When I encouraged him to tell me more, he described paying our local taxes in a municipal office attached to an elementary school.

"Walking down the hall I was surrounded by what we never got to experience," he said. "The little desks and the coat hooks two feet off the ground and the construction paper art decorating the hall. It made me sad. I tried to imagine you and me sitting at the desk of little Pammie or Alex Junior during parent night, going to the gym for recitals. It was a visceral reminder of what we'll never have and well, it sucked. A part of me wanted to get out of there as fast as possible."

During the worst of my early coping days I found myself irritated by the little tykes. Being annoyed with them somehow made being around them easier. My logic at the time seemed to be: if I didn't connect and bond with them, then the pain of not having my own would be alleviated a bit. I was an anti-kid woman who wanted nothing more than to have kids. A bit of a paradox, wouldn't you say?

Then I'd sneak a glimpse of someone's Junior at a social gathering, his jack o' lantern smile innocently gazing up at me and, well, I'd melt inside. *Oh Junior*, I'd think, *you're not the one I need to hold accountable for my inability to conceive. You're just a sweet-faced little guy who has to make his own way in this world, and like any innocent child, you'll need all the help and hard-won knowledge of us bigger people.*

In time and with some effort on my part, a subtle transformation occurred. When I'd catch a child gazing up at me in grocery stores or airports, I'd meet their look and return it with a smile rather than look away in pain as had been my natural instinct. They'd smile back and we'd share a happy moment. The new thought bubble over my head: *I may be barren but that doesn't mean I can't appreciate a beautiful, innocent child.*

After the experiences of IVF or "pregnancy lite," the challenge became looking at little ones and not comparing them to what our children might have been doing at the same age. There were three little girls who tested me in that way. The first had a pageboy haircut and the defiant attitude expected of a little girl with two older brothers. The second had the natural curiosity and disposition of a leader that comes with being the eldest child and protector of two younger siblings. The third, the youngest of the three, had just turned five. She had an angelic smile, long golden locks and the confident, slightly demanding demeanor of an only child used to getting her own way.

These girls had little in common with each other outside of closeness in age, but they each tugged on my heartstrings in a special way that would forever bind them together. They were each conceived and delivered the same year to friends and extended family at the same time I was giving it my all and then some in my last best effort at getting pregnant. While my precious embies, valiant as they were to make it to transfer day, didn't go the distance, these precious girls – all conceived unexpectedly – did. And what a reminder they were of what might have been. I saw them intermittently and when I did I couldn't help but study them closely and wonder. How could I not? Their mothers' pregnancies were forever engraved in my memory. Their birth announcements and every milestone that had come since were potent symbols. To them I was just Auntie Pam, but the intense connection and the visceral emotions these three evoked will stay with me, always.

Not long after seeing Goldilocks, the youngest of the three, I made my way to a file cabinet in the house where a few years earlier I had stored my medical files. I rummaged through a dog-eared manila folder and found what I was looking for. Captured in a grainy image were the first three embryos. I was transported to an imaginary world where they actually made their way through to full gestation and became fully-formed triplets. Two other slips of shiny paper contained the other images – the two sets of twins. I played with an idea of what it would have been like to have one or more starting school. I paused for a moment. It was astonishing to think that they'd be well beyond potty training and demonstrating sometimes defiant independence.

"You would have been Rhodes scholars – all of you. That I'm certain," I said wistfully as I tucked the photos safely back in my file.

Very early the next morning a haunting melody filled my head. In my dream the little souls we tried to create had escaped this planet into the warm and ethereal world that lay beyond. It was a vivid dream. I was floating high above the earth as soft clouds rolled by. On the horizon the sun was just beginning to rise. The dawn sky was a soft pink. Around me the most glorious sound could be heard. It was the cooing and laughter of happy children and under that sound was the gorgeous accompaniment of string instruments. It was the moving music we had heard from Spanish composer Joaquin Rodrigo growing louder as the sun made its appearance in the distance. There could not have been a more serene scene imaginable.

I awakened, for once, with my mind at peace.

SECTION III:
FINDING MY VOICE

CHAPTER EIGHT

ACCEPTANCE: OWN IT BECAUSE YOU CAN'T CHANGE IT

Are you there God? It's me, Pamela. I have a few things to say. I know I haven't been the best Catholic – in fact, I'm not sure if I'm still even considered Catholic. It's been like fifteen years since my last confession. Not sure what exactly I've done to piss you off so mightily – maybe it was something in a previous life? But I'd like to ask for your forgiveness. I know it's not for me to say, but I think I've paid my price, served my sentence, completed my penance. And, if it's not too much to ask, I'd like to have a little more strength and some peace, oh, and a lot more understanding and less insensitivity from your other, you know, more fertile children. That's not too much to ask, is it?

And another thing. Can you send some new playmates my way? It would be really nice to have some people who know what I've lived through, some peers who can make me feel less, well, weird. In the meantime, I'll try to live in the moment. In fact, I see the fridge is empty. Let me do something about that.

In hindsight, I should have chosen a different activity. The grocery store is an infertile woman's special hell. I was reminded of that when the automatic doors opened into the produce section. There I was checking out the asparagus, feeling all evolved and ready to start a new chapter in my life – one that would not dwell on my infertility. And then BAM. Around the corner hidden behind a mountain of freshly picked peaches stood a very pregnant woman caressing her full belly.

Really, God? This how you reward me for trying to turn over a new leaf?

No need to torment myself further catching views of her hard-to-miss swollen belly so I consciously kept my eyes focused shoulder height as the very pregnant shopper made her way through produce. Phew! I made it to the dairy section, but who was waiting for me? Yet *another* pregnant woman was rubbing her belly as she stood contemplating her yogurt choices. What the? Did I *not* get the memo? Is this the equivalent of Hat Day at a minor league baseball game? Surely today must be "Just-About-to-Go-into-Labor" day at Whole Foods.

At a minimum there must be a baby boomlet taking place. This prega-palooza can't just be my imagination – or was it, I wondered. I had to know so I did a little research on my return and in the safety of my home. The answer? It depends on which study you want to read. Apparently a boomlet *was* taking place, according to a study from the CDC, which was covered in one newspaper with this headline: "Record Number of Infants Born in U.S. in 2007." Ah ha! I knew it. But then, hold on, how does that explain an even more recent report out from the U.S. Census Bureau? "More Women Are Having Fewer Children, If at All."

"In the last 30 years, the number of women aged 40 to 44 with no children has doubled, from 10 percent to 20 percent. And those who are mothers have an average of 1.9 children each, more than one child fewer than women of the same age in 1976."

There can be only one explanation. Clearly the census takers were not spending enough time at the grocery store.

Another surreal activity for infertiles? Visiting historical locations like palaces, for instance. It was hard to miss the importance of progeny – and the inevitable mulling over what my life would have been like in a different time and place – when surrounded by larger-than-life portraits depicting the lineage of once powerful rulers. Their very future and ability to exert influence depended on successfully mating and reproducing. The piercing eyes staring down at me from ornate walls brought to mind a scene in the HBO series *Rome*. I cringed when I heard Cleopatra whisper to Caesar, "A man with no sons has no future."

Sure, it was the twenty-first century but the sentiment held. In countries with declining birth rates there were generous incentives to encourage baby-making. The pro-natalistic policies might not always work to encourage large families, but the fact that they were in place said something about the value of fertility – and sent a clear message to those who couldn't conceive. It was hard not to feel, well, devalued.

On my way out of visiting one grand house on one trip overseas I had a new appreciation for Japan's Princess Masako and the intense pressure she faced to produce an heir. It's hard enough to deal with the heartbreak of infertility in private, quite another to have to face it along with the judgment and disappointment of prying eyes – whether in the 1700s or today. The world's palaces may be emptying out but it seemed we still had a long way to go to shake loose those crusty but powerful views from the past.

Much as I tried to fit in with the mommies and daddies who surrounded me, I continued to find myself the odd woman out – the proverbial square peg in the round hole. Infertility was no longer something those closest to me had the interest or fortitude to discuss. Can't imagine why on earth that was. I mean, the Sisyphean topic clearly still fascinated me, but they had moved on – mostly deeper into their parenting communities. Me? I still craved hard-to-find understanding and a different kind of community. I couldn't be the only non-mom feeling that way. So one particularly lonesome evening in early 2007 I sent out a call over the Internet.

"Hello. I'm new to this but your blog post really spoke to me. I've just started my own blog called *Coming2Terms.*"

Ping. A return comment arrived almost immediately from across the Pacific Ocean in Australia. "I'm sorry we had to meet under these circumstances but I'm glad you found me."

I couldn't believe it. I checked out the Aussie's blogroll and found it full of women from around the globe who wrote about exactly what I was thinking, what I felt, what I was living with. I sent out another message. Ping. And another. Heartfelt comments began regularly filling my

Yahoo inbox from Pretoria, South Africa; St. Louis, Missouri; London; Rabat, Morocco; Toronto, Canada; Baltimore, Maryland; Newton, Massachusetts; Singapore; Houston, Texas; Phoenix, Arizona; Pasig City, The Philippines; Gainesville, Virginia; Wilber, Nebraska; Broenshoej, Denmark; Huntsville, Alabama; Kernersville, North Carolina; West Midlands, England; Ann Arbor, Michigan; Vincennes, France; Temple, Florida; Gauteng, South Africa; New Orleans; Sofia, Bulgaria; Slovenia; and more.

Pretty soon I was overwhelmed in a very good way. I was far from alone. Some of the women were newly diagnosed with conception problems, others were veterans. Some faced primary infertility, some were singletons or lesbian couples who wanted to conceive, some were struggling with a "male factor," others secondary infertility. Finally I had found my tribe! Posts were spilling out of my head. Women I could relate to and understand. These women rocked. We got down to some serious bonding, venting, comforting. It was like getting wrapped up in a warm blanket. It was blog therapy.

I felt like I had been released from solitary confinement. Maybe in light of what happened after my first post, the better analogy would be that of a starved person who gorged the first time they saw food. I actually got nauseous. I didn't sleep much the night I put up my first blog post. That's because it was the *first* time I had acknowledged publicly that I was INFERTILE. I was blogging semi-anonymously using my first and middle name, Pamela Jeanne, so it wasn't like putting my Social Security number, photo and phone number online but it was dizzying nonetheless to disclose something I had been socialized to hide.

I didn't get all the hype about bloggers and the communities they were forming until I suited up. Now I knew what the big deal was. For the first time in a very long time I felt at home, among my people. I became all but a blog addict. I had to read what was happening with *Weebles Wobblog, Stirrup Queens* and so, so many others. Early mornings had once been quiet time for Alex and I to sip on coffee and discuss the world's latest stories captured in newsprint. We were old school and still had a paper delivered to our house even though the Internet updated headlines by the minute. Now I was caught up in a series of different dramas. My own – and those of women who were part of a much larger and familiar cast. They joined me on a new sort of stage. We could finish each other's sentences. Their comments were like tonics. Some that stood out:

"I am sure that most people believe we have 'moved on,' and sometimes I can even believe that myself, but then something will happen to remind me that the shadow of infertility still looms large in my life, and probably always will. I have often said this – I hate, absolutely hate, knowing that people feel sorry for me because we don't have kids. I hate being the object of pity. I want them to know that we're OK, the world didn't come to an end, I'm not about to throw myself off a cliff, etc. But at the same time, just because I'm not standing at the cliff's edge, I don't want them thinking that our life is peachy keen either, and that we don't keenly feel the absence of a child in our life, every single day."

"Thanks so much for sharing [an] amazing articulation of the grief of infertility. Through my two losses I have tried, repeatedly, to explain to my fertile friends the nature of IF [infertility] and miscarriage grief - how it is different from the loss of a friend or family member. In particular, people have a hard time grasping onto the cyclical nature of IF and m/c [miscarriage] grief. They make assumptions about your recovery and are bewildered when your grief raises its ugly head over and over. Your writing has repeatedly provided me with the words I have such a hard time finding."

"Just wanted to wish you well and say you're absolutely right. Putting on that game face takes strength and courage. It's a fertile, fertile world out there."

Alex, meanwhile, had overnight become an infertility blogger widower. He had a mixed response to my newfound hobby. On the one hand he was relieved I was finding an outlet for my pent-up thoughts and emotions, but suddenly each morning he found me locked in what amounted to a love affair with my laptop. Now that he was a blogger widower I teased him.

"I know I'm a tough act to follow, but if I ever get hit by a beer truck, you have my permission to marry someone like Princess12. I see you with someone who challenges you, makes you think, makes you laugh."

"Please avoid beer trucks."

"Seriously, you could also marry Cora or Lucy. All are a variation on me, so they've got my approval."

"Hmmm." (Alex was clearly trying to imagine being married to them).

"Okay. Who can I marry?"

"This is a weird conversation." He was clearly stalling.

"I know I'm a lot to handle..."

"That's an understatement."

"Names, please."

"Pammie, it's just it takes a lot of man to well, you know..."

"I'm that bad?"

"No. It's just I see myself as a Ferrari mechanic. Ferraris are beautiful but temperamental cars that need a lot of tinkering. When it runs, it runs like nothing else." Alex sighed with appreciation. "But when it doesn't ..."

That explains more than my personality. Maybe I should have gone to a Ferrari shop instead of the RE clinic. I rationalized that by immersing myself in a new crucible, this one online, I would emerge a stronger, happier mate. Alex was relieved to learn that my emotional see-sawing was not isolated. My "sisters" were echoing my thoughts. We were singing a common chorus.

But I also recognized that I needed to tread lightly in this new territory. I was, after all, a newly-diagnosed infertile woman's worst nightmare. I mean, there I was north of forty and, after running the infertility treatment gauntlet with most if not all of the treatments – conventional and unconventional, eastern and western medicine – I had failed to fall pregnant. I would have avoided me like the plague ten years earlier. Too much like the grim reaper. I knew I had to do more than just dwell on my failure, so I tried to promote understanding. Given the power of search engines, I knew I'd also likely get hits and visits from the random woman searching for pregnancy-related information. My most provocative post was couched as a social experiment. It went like this:

> One of the techniques used to highlight what it's like to walk in someone else's shoes is to "role play." Well, I'd like to take that a step further. I'd like to invite my fertility-challenged readers as well as the moms who drop by to participate. Cue the music (you know the tune) and now, let's enter the *Twilight Zone*...
>
> Everyone fighting infertility, you are now able to conceive – the natural way. Those of you with children, those who conceived without a thought as to ovulation cycles, FSH or sperm counts, you are now mysteriously unable to bear children. The little ones you once nursed, cuddled and bragged on at social gatherings, they are mysteriously gone – this is the *Twilight Zone*. The realization of childlessness is frightening, devastating because the once fertile now find themselves in a house suddenly silent -- no more giggles or playful chatter or background noise courtesy of *Dora the Explorer* or *Sesame Street*. Those who were once infertile are equally in disbelief. They've just had a loving and spontaneous romp. Two weeks later two pink lines magically appear on an at-home pregnancy kit. The newly pregnant can't quite wrap their heads around the idea that no external intervention was required... not a pill, not a shot, not even a visit to a doctor's office. Now, mysteriously pregnant, the once infertile are wondering if they can muster the confidence to hold a baby shower or whether it might jinx the prospects for a successful delivery. Meanwhile, those who have come to the realization that their plumbing doesn't work are

desperate. It's slowly dawning on them that the spare bedrooms in their house might, at best, only serve as guest rooms. With the scene set, some newly fertile women (remember we're living in opposite land) meet their now infertile women friends for lunch. What's their conversation? How does the dialogue develop? How do their relationships change? The story is now in your hands.

The responses to this blog post confirmed my suspicions:

"Oh, I love this *Twilight Zone*. The realisation of what it would be like slowly dawned on me as I read your post. To conceive naturally, to have a normal pregnancy and a healthy baby at the end? Wow. I am basking in the glow, just basking. My own baby? Really? Really? Really? And unfortunately, the little mean part of me is also glad that the fertile community would get to experience what it means when your body fails you inexplicably. I hope I would be gentle with the previously in-fertile. I hope I would be able to sit down over a cup of coffee and say, "How are you doing? Are you ok?" I hope I would be able to encourage a friend without telling her about this woman I know who tried and tried and eventually went on holiday and drank bergamote tea and fell pregnant and now has four children. I hope I would be able to be there with her, to share the experience without diminishing it or increasing her guilt. I think I would limit my children's entry into our friendship, I wouldn't talk about [my little one's] cute smiles or how difficult I am finding it to lose weight. I hope I would be a friend who remains me and who doesn't metamorphise into a Mother. (Oh, so much bitterness I bear against mothers. Would I be able to control it in the *Twilight Zone*. I hope so.)"

"I think this post should be printed and posted in the break room in every office and read at the neighborhood brunch. It MIGHT give the fertiles a teeny clue about the desperation and feelings of emptiness and possibly prevent them from saying some of the stupid things they say. I personally have been on both sides of the fence and trust me, infertility is not the better of the two sides."

"Totally love this idea. I'd love to believe that I'd take the moral high ground, too, and just say, how are you? is there anything I can do? Because I think if you've been through this you really genuinely don't want anyone else to suffer. Maybe I'd have an inward moment of *schadenfreude*, but I'd limit myself to that, I hope."

"What would they say? Or what do I wish they'd say? I wish they'd say: "I had no idea it was like this, I am sorry." And "I don't know how you managed to keep going such a long time while dealing with this." And, perhaps, "I'm sorry. I didn't get it. Now I do." I think I would be too stunned to do anything. Of course, I'm still so raw from finding out I have to do IVF. I always worried about multiples due to family history - and hemorrhaging - and miscarriage - but not even being able to get pregnant? I was always taught that if you asked someone if they had children and they didn't you apologized for the question. Of course, I have relatives who never had children for a variety of reasons. There are so many ways I just cannot relate to others experiences outside of the intense pain of this experience."

"My hope would be that I would remember to just say "I'm sorry," and leave it at that. But, we are all so human, so flawed, would I actually gloat? I don't know. I honestly don't know."

"It's such an interesting idea because I have a feeling I'd be going on and on about how amazed I am that I've conceived--with little thought to how the other person is taking it (now newly non-parenting and infertile themselves). On the other hand, I would like to think that the experience has affected me enough that I remain circumspect even in my surprise. I don't know if I'd ever be able to have the baby shower. I think I'd still be freaked out."

"I'm sure I would not behave nicely. I'd be a blithering fool, yipping on with joy. But I also couldn't make it through a pregnancy calmly, because it's not just about IF for me, it's about high risk pregnancy."

"I've been giving this a lot of thought and then I realized why I was having a hard time figuring out what the conversation would be like. I would be so shocked that I conceived with my eggs that I would be speechless. Then I would remain speechless for fear that it wasn't true and that I have finally gone insane."

"Since it looks like I'm one of the only ones to be on the fertile/now infertile side, I can only say what I have been saying as this is happening in my real world now. I get told that if I have faith it will happen. I tell her that she doesn't have to enjoy being pregnant. I say I'm sorry for the 100th time for telling her if they just had sex everyday they would finally get pregnant. She tells me that I at least have the one to be grateful for. We both then stare silently at our half-empty plates and take a drink from our glasses. I'm drinking wine. She's drinking water with a wedge of lemon. At the shower, I pretend to have to tie my shoe so I don't have to touch the miniature clothing being passed around. She tries to steer her mother away from me for fear that she will ask me when I will have another baby. We both cry. For each other. For ourselves."

"I started to type my answer, but then I saw a problem in the question. I have kids now, via IVF, but I still consider myself infertile. Even if I mysteriously conceived through ordinary, everyday sex, having been through the shots and the heartbreak, and everything that comes with infertility, I would still be infertile. I'm not sure that my response to my friend would change that much from what it would be now, or two years ago."

"I've been trying to think about how to reply to this. I think I'd have to actively quash a smug sense of having got my revenge. But I think that would be fairly fleeting. Would I feel guilty about achieving pregnancy so easily whilst watching other women suffer? I think again those feelings would be tempered by a sense of things have "evened themselves out". I think I would feel bad for the newly-infertile, but in a "well, honey, that's life, now you know" kind of way."

"I'd like to think I would move on to a state of mind where I could offer genuine support for the newly infertile. Go out there by day and be sensitive and sympathetic, then come home at night and be just overjoyed by my new-found good fortune."

"I'm one of the fertiles, and, truthfully, I can't even imagine what it would be like not to have my boys. My husband and I did discuss "what ifs", as in "what would we do if it doesn't happen for us" when we decided we wanted children (because we were "older" and understood the potential), but I'm not sure we really, really grasped what it would mean if we landed on the other side of the divide. As a fair number of friends have. And I'm not sure what it would have done to our relationship."

"I'm not infertile, though I did have an endoscopy for endometriosis at 18, and spent ten years worrying I would be. At the same time, as someone not exposed much to infertility as a child growing up, I think I went into a lot of conversations in my early years uninformed. While we fertiles need to be more aware of what comes out of our mouths, I also think those who are working at pregnancy should realize that not everyone makes a comment or talks about their baby or pregnancy to hurt someone. You think about what's going on in your life. If you want to be shielded from that conversation, you need to say something. Just as I have to say something when I hear a mother tell her daughter she looks fat. It's a process of education. We all have our hot buttons. I don't mean for this to sound insensitive, but I don't think the dialogue will change unless we are honest with each other when a comment or conversation stings."

Amen! And, fertile girlfriends, I'm screwing up my courage to be more forthright. It's just I totally hate crying in public and being the human equivalent of the Old Faithful geyser. I don't think I'm ready just yet to let it all hang out. But, just so you know, as much as I revel in the camaraderie of women who have walked in my shoes, hearing from nice, naturally-occurring mothers like you also makes me happy – 'cause I think one day we might, you know, hang out or something.

Now that I was unleashing all sorts of pent-up thoughts, I started waking up with a sense of contentedness that had long eluded me. Not happy to let me off the hook just yet, the universe threw a few more curve balls to see if I'd evolved sufficiently. Have you ever noticed how when you're highly attuned to a subject, you can't seem to get away from it – much as you might want to? For me that ranged from cats and dogs (while I would like one very much, animal dander allergies make them lethal to my lungs, so how was it they always sought me out?) to pregnant women who still seemed to cluster around me like metal filaments to a magnet.

For example, I was on a *Thelma and Louise*-like adventure with a gal pal who also didn't have any kids. Let me be clear – there was to be no driving a car off a cliff. In fact, we were the "G" rated version of these feisty gals. No crimes had been or would be committed. It had been a laidback, indulgent weekend starting with a convertible car ride experience of wind in the hair and singing loudly, if a little off key, to tunes blaring on the radio.

We spent Friday in a two-person float making our way down a mountain snow-fed river for three hours, followed by rum punches and lunch at a noisy, sunshine drenched outdoor restaurant by the river. We made it back in time to nap, shower and head over with a picnic basket full of wine, fruit, cheese and salami to catch an outdoor performance of *The Taming of the Shrew* (how appropriate was that?) on the beachfront of Lake Tahoe.

"Louise" had gone on ahead to find a place on the sand for our blanket. When I found her she was happily engaged in a conversation with another Shakespeare fan. Now let me say that Louise and I had different opinions on the whole pregnancy and baby thing. Where I'd struggled with anger, resentment and other not so nice feelings toward those who conceived and their newborns, she was not bothered in the least by their success. A role model to be sure. So, who had captured Louise's attention?

"Thelma," she said, "this woman is nine and half months pregnant! Can you believe it?"

"Well," I replied somewhat grumpily, not at all happy with the idea of sharing my carefree, childfree weekend with anyone remotely child*ful*, "I hope you don't have any plans for changing that tonight, 'cause I don't think we'll be in a position to help."

I also noticed that out of the seven women seated directly in front of us, at least one of them was pregnant, too. Louise continued to merrily chat up the couple while we waited for the performance to begin. I, meanwhile, poured myself a very large glass of wine.

"What are you planning to name the child?" Louise quizzed the jolly father-to-be while his wife took one of many trips to the ladies room.

He enthusiastically responded, "Well, if it's a girl, it could be Emma Elise and if it's a boy it could be Sean Arthur. We've practiced yelling both out loud in the car to see if they work."

We both laughed at his cheerful good humor. I began to soften a bit. He was clearly going to be a great father. His wife waddled back and tried to get comfortable. I looked at her in a whole new light as well. She was rubbing her belly and quietly sat back to enjoy what would surely be one of the last quiet nights in her life for a while.

As the sun made its way down behind the tree line it occurred to me that Louise actually had the right idea. I would never in a million years at that point in my life have engaged this couple sitting next to us in conversation. In fact, I would have avoided them like the plague and likely found somewhere else to throw a blanket. Instead, I was able to appreciate that avoiding people based on pregnancy alone, while a good defense mechanism at times, doesn't have to be a lifelong impulse. I needed to shed my prejudices. I wondered if my fertile counterparts were capable or willing to do the same about my people.

I admit I hung out in what amounts to infertility rehab for an extended stay. No sign of the usual celebs in this rehab. It's more like a monastery, self-service in nature. There is not, to my knowledge, a twelve-step process for getting the upper hand with infertility. So that left me no choice but to make one up.

1. **Acknowledge that you can't get pregnant the "old school" way** – it doesn't seem to matter how many candles have been lit, whether the mood-setting or the spiritual kind.

2. **Consult an army of specialists** – you've followed advice found in books, online or compliments of old wives tales to no avail; proceed to Western-medicine-staffed fertility clinics eager to sell you services.

3. **Spend boatloads of money on treatments with low percentages of success** – meanwhile your friends procreate like mad, remodel their homes, buy new cars and otherwise stimulate the economy.

4. **Explore the Eastern practice of medicine** – why not? Leave no stone unturned.

5. **Avoid malls, parks and any child-themed locale** – there's no need to subject yourself unnecessarily to that which you cannot seem to have.

6. **Buy a ticket to denial** – any place is preferable to the reality of Infertility Land.

7. **Declare war on all smug parents** – these thoughtless creatures are to be avoided at all costs.

8. **Withdraw from social obligations that revolve around other people's children** – self-preservation becomes essential at this stage.

9. **Exit the infertility treatment maze** – you're tired of running into dead ends; arrive at either successful treatment, look into adoption, or live without children

10. **Keep a journal or start a blog** – express your thoughts and properly vent your pent-up emotions.

11. **Hang out in infertility rehab** – slowly attempt to re-engage and co-exist with friends and colleagues and their child-filled lives ... perhaps write a book?

12. **Fully re-enter society** – accept that you're forever changed by infertility but know that society, largely, will never fully understand what you have been through and/or continue to battle. (*Warning: re-entry can be exacerbated by those who don't give a flying fig about infertility's lasting or collateral damage.*)

Ultimately, though, and aided with the efforts of patient, kind-hearted family and loyal friends, I realized I needed to emerge from rehab and learn how to cope, to live among fertiles. I needed to lose my fortress mentality. I started slowly, first, venturing out into malls again. Then I opened to socializing – complete with strangers, even. One night Alex and I arrived on Stanford's campus for the fortieth birthday party of a professor with whom I had collaborated on a history-making DARPA robot car project called "Stanley." (I must add that making regular trips to Stanford's campus during that year-long robot car project wasn't easy, given how much time I'd spent there for my more personal and fruitless Stanley project.) The party crowd ranged from people in their mid-twenties to fifty-somethings – Silicon Valley at its best and most diverse.

The host professor and his wife were fairly new in our social circle. While they, too, were without children, we had never broached the subject of how or why that was. I assumed, given their ages, that they, like us, were unable to have kids. It was oddly comforting when we first met to think Alex and I could expand our circle of friends with a couple, well, more like us. We'd be free to get together spontaneously without concerns like babysitter availability, and discuss topics that didn't involve diaper duty, pre-school selections and the like. I had been hoping at some point to have a heart-to-heart and compare our histories, but the time had never been right. Come to think of it, there probably never is a convenient time to bring up the "I" word. Five minutes into the fortieth birthday party the hostess pulled me aside, her face glowing, to share her news. They were celebrating more than forty – they were *finally* expecting. You know, she told me, with great relief, "We kept waiting and waiting and it wasn't happening, until now anyway!" She was due in December.

I hugged her, of course, asked how she was feeling. I joked with her and her husband about what they would name their child. I had the drill down. I was not about to rain on their parade. In the back of my head as I gushed along with them, I couldn't help but think *there goes another one, graduating and moving on.* Not so very long before that, the news would have flattened me. So, while caught sidewise and awash in mixed feelings – *do I get drunk and over-indulge in the chocolate-y desserts or accept this as just one more cosmic joke from the universe? SURPRISE!* – I found myself feeling more wistful than anything else. So much for those spontaneous, child-free get-togethers.

I wasn't the only one making adjustments and observations. Alex had a few insights, too, like the one in Germany when I was accompanying him on a work commitment

"You know how you've always wondered about whether people who don't have children can ever fully 'grow up'?" he asked.

"Mmm, yes."

"Well I've been thinking about that," he added as he reached for slice of brown bread and cheese. "That, and whether there's a way – outside of parenting – to qualify as different but equally bona fide adults."

"And?"

"We get older, sure, but people in our shoes also stay a different kind of young. We see the world another way

"You can say *that* again!"

"And because we can't have kids our lives are not as predictable. That's why people younger than us like having us as friends – we're not like their parents."

"Oh, you mean because we relate to them more as peers?"

"Yeah. There's no paternalistic attitude. We don't talk down to them – no 'just wait until you have kids' talk from us. You know, Pammie, people like us, people who can't have kids…we're living our own kind of normal. *This* is our normal. This is what our life is supposed to be."

Alex opened his arms in a sweeping gesture as if the statement needed greater emphasis.

Our conversation came after eight hours of heavenly sleep in the wake of twenty hours traveling from San Francisco through Frankfurt and into Stuttgart. We talked in a café over one of the best cups of coffee ever served, but what I valued even more than the caffeine were the insights that came with it.

That's when it became clear to me. I had spent the better part of my adult life in a losing battle by allowing other people and traditions to dictate what was "normal," to let their ideas define me and my life. I had been torturing myself – trapped as an infertile in a fertile world. Sad as I was about our losses and not succeeding with pregnancy, I knew that my grieving was pretty well worked out. But, I faced another challenge – that of feeling like a perennial outsider. There was clearly no way I would ever succeed in being "one of them" – an innocent who one day woke up and said, "*Whaddya say, honey? Let's get pregnant.*" And then did.

In order to truly come to terms with infertility I had to stop using the fertile world as a measuring stick. I would forever be an alien if I had stayed in that mindset. It was a difficult lesson to learn, but a liberating one after years of feeling inadequate and unable to fulfill the life I thought I was supposed to be leading. I'm not suggesting that the ten-plus years associated with trying to conceive and the hoping for a miraculous pregnancy was a mistake. Far from it. In fact, I can only be at peace knowing we did our best to have children with what was available to us, pursuing the science that we were comfortable pursuing.

Alex reminded me of the line in the movie *Whale Rider* when the young Maori girl observed about the way life turned out, "It's not good. It's not bad, it's just what happened."

I was still wrapping my head around that sentiment as we made our way to Ireland for the holidays.

———————————

"How old is your daughter?"

The woman behind the pharmacy counter in Dublin caught me off guard. I was flummoxed. I instinctively looked around to see if she was talking to someone else. Then it hit me.

It was more like getting access to a private club. It was as though I had been magically transported into an infertile's parallel universe – the mommy and daddy universe.

The thought bubble over my head filled with questions and exclamations: *"You can't really be talking to me? Are you? Wow, you are! You think I'm the mom!"*

That's right. The pharmacist had completely ignored my brother-in-law after he indicated that my niece needed a stronger type of cough syrup to combat some cold/flu symptoms. The pharmacist had focused her attention, laser-like, on me. She calmly repeated her question. "Now, how old is your daughter?"

I blushed, a small part of me wanting to hold on to the moment as long as possible. My brother-in-law, distracted by the rows and rows of cough syrups lining the shelves, responded immediately, "Eight. She's eight."

I nodded in agreement. The pharmacist's gaze didn't move from my direction. "Does she have a dry cough or does it sound like congestion?"

There was no point in correcting her – as if it would matter in this instance. "There's a bit of rumble, but it's mostly dry," I responded, knowing well my own cough. I had picked it up, too, after my niece had covered me in spontaneous hugs and kisses in the few days since our arrival. Earlier in the afternoon my brother-in-law had handed the little cuddle bug off to the responsible parents of another little girl who was celebrating her birthday with a group movie viewing involving ten of her best friends, half of whom were also sniffling, coughing and sneezing between their squeals and giggles. It was cold and flu season after all.

Back in my own house the following week in cozy sweats, sipping tea and fighting the cotton candy in my brain (compliments of jetlag and cold medicine), I was struck once again by how easy it is for the world at large to naturally assume that all adults of a certain age are parents of some kind. There's nothing to indicate otherwise. And that's part of the difficulty in trying to explain the infertile's experience of living in a parallel universe, and then there are the plain and simply uncomfortable moments, which take us back to where my story began.

The venture firm where I worked had arranged a casual dinner as part of a Napa Valley offsite (I know, there are worse places to have an offsite). Among those seated at a long table were people newer to the office. As with any meal that had an element of team-building to it, there was lots of small talk exploring non-work topics. With most everyone on hand in their forties or early fifties there were abundant stories about children and the challenges of parenting. During one awkward moment a question came my way, lobbed over two or three others, aimed at involving me in a group discussion at the other end of the table.

"Pamela, you have, what two boys? Or is it a boy and a girl? So you know what it's like to..."

I cut him off immediately, startled and confused by the question: "I don't have any children."

"But you have pictures on your desk of you and children..."

"They're my nieces and nephews..." I replied, attempting to clarify.

"Oh, so you don't have kids?"

"No ... no kids," I said.

There was a minor pause before the person to my immediate left, the managing partner whom I long suspected knew more about my infertility than he had let on, jumped in and redirected the conversation to save me further embarrassment. It took me back to the time when I needed time away from the office for surgery. Over lunch he had asked about my scheduled time off. I made a vague reference to a laparoscopy assuming he didn't know what it was. More tuned in than most men, he said gently, trying to be helpful, "Um, so I've heard that couples who don't have children have happier marriages."

But the others at dinner were clueless. I wanted very much to elaborate, to tell them that my husband I had spent a decade trying to conceive, that we'd pursued outside help at a research hospital, that we'd passed all of the tests with flying colors but flunked the final exam – more than once. But with the waiter bringing our entrees and the din of the restaurant and the buzz kill associated with my story, it just didn't seem appropriate then and there to open up my life to them. Instead I was left feeling frustrated and closeted. And that's where a quote from an article about blogging infertility came into play. I had been contacted by a journalist to provide some perspective on what it was like to be part of a growing community of infertility bloggers. The reporter relayed my thoughts this way:

"...many never tell their family or friends that they're undergoing treatment, or only tell them after treatment is over. "It really is a double-edged sword," Tsigdinos says. And, perversely, it's a dilemma made more complicated by modern technology. "I often wonder," she says, "Was it harder to be infertile in the Fifties [than today]? Because in the Fifties, at my age, people would say, 'Gee, they couldn't have children' because birth control, the Pill, didn't exist.... Today, there's more ambiguity. People don't know if you elected not to have children, if you couldn't have children, if we made the 'mistake' of waiting too long."

And that ambiguity challenged me more and more as I grew older. I didn't want to make a federal case about what Alex and I had lived through (*okay, yeah, I get the hypocrisy of that statement given this book*), but I also hated the usually wrong assumptions that came with my childless circumstances. Why, I wondered, did we infertile folk feel it necessary to go out of our way to protect others from the reality of our experiences, to suffer silently wishing we had a repertoire of our own child-related stories to tell? Well, we do actually have plenty of stories but they're more clinical in nature.

For a split second at dinner I considered telling it like it truly was – but then what? Given the sensitive nature of the subject matter, I had to weigh the risks of sharing my story with what might come next. Would my colleagues find my honesty inappropriate? Would they resent me for trapping them at a table with a topic sure to make them uncomfortable? Would they feel an obligation to ask more questions and offer unsolicited advice? Or worse yet, would they make light of it, dismiss it and move on to a more congenial topic?

I certainly never aspired to be an infertility community "poster child," but I was beyond frustrated at living in a society that preferred people in my situation be silent, invisible. Earlier, in the mixer part of the evening, I had to smile prettily and nod quietly when a colleague directly across from me gloated as he savored a glass of wine. "When my four children – all now gone from the nest – come back together for a family dinner, well, I'm just at my happiest – God, take me now! My kids, they're everything to me." And turning to a colleague who had just finished describing her two children, he asked, "Wouldn't you agree?"

That's when I had to escape to the ladies room. The only trouble was I couldn't live in the stall all night. The truth is people living with infertility don't like living in a vacuum. We flock to our blogging community to talk about those things that we don't have liberty to discuss in our day-to-day lives. But many of our experiences deserve a fair and wider hearing. We represent up to fourteen percent of society after all – one in eight couples of child-bearing age. Yet there are no walkathons, golf tournaments, fundraisers, or consistent celebrity-led efforts to raise awareness and understanding about the topic.

Quite the opposite, in fact. Most try to hide it. There have been a few brave souls who unabashedly acknowledged that their conception required outside involvement like Courteney Cox, Brooke Shields, and two of the three Dixie Chicks (Martie McGuire and Emily Robison). The Internet, meanwhile, buzzed with twisted, almost gleeful speculation about who actually might have had to rely on treatment but never acknowledged it. The *schadenfreude* implications made my skin crawl. *She's a beautiful, successful – (fill in the blank TV star, singer, model) – but heh, heh, heh, she's deficieeeent!*

How backward would our understanding about Parkinson's disease be without the likes of Michael J. Fox or Muhammad Ali? Or what about Alzheimer's disease if not for the honesty of Ronald Reagan or Sandra Day O'Connor's family?

I can hear the protests already, Who the hell cares? Nobody is, like, *dying* as a result of infertility. True, it's not fatal, but it is a life sentence, and while everyone hears about the wildly successful treatments – usually in the form of a starting basketball squad – they're far from representative of what most infertile couples experience. And we may not die from it but on the *very* worst days, you either want to die or you feel like you're losing your mind. If fertility or virility ain't no big *thang* then why do doctors counsel patients undergoing radiation or chemo to freeze their sperm or eggs? The muted voices of the infertile only serve to perpetuate the shame and stigma.

I can't help but appreciate how much I must seem like the Holly Hunter character in *Broadcast News*, who started every morning with a good cry. After all my gnashing of teeth and weeping I should be fully dehydrated by now, right? One evening tears came to me again, but not for the usual reasons. These were tears of relief – so, so much better than tears of sadness. They came in the wake of what felt like a tremor around my heart. I had been reading a book about coping with loss and how the darker emotions, grief, despair and fear, could actually be helpful rather than hurtful. The author made the case that it was important to embrace the dark emotions rather than to fight them. As I relaxed and meditated a bit on the idea, I felt a release of pent-up energy – and with it – some of the pain that had been tightly wound up inside me.

I hadn't realized until the jolt just how much fighting my anger, sadness and loss had been holding me back. I'd like to tell you there was an easy route to that moment, but that would be lying. I hadn't been smoking anything funny nor having a peyote moment. No, I slowly realized that submitting to the pain, not trying to control or deny it, was the first step to healing.

Now I am usually as skeptical as anyone when I hear someone tell me that they've "pushed through." At the same time I was able to see that I had been working overtime to protect myself from further pain. The intense sorrow of not getting to meet the little souls we tried to create had been so severe that I did everything possible to avoid becoming so vulnerable again. In the process I had also closed myself off from feeling, deeply, the good emotions that come with an open heart. Why would I want to connect so deeply and incur the risk of such yawning hurt? Because I wanted to feel the good things deeply once again, too. My head was still caught up in trying to understand why some mothers and fathers happened by chance while others never got the same chance, but my heart wanted to live again. More hard work still lay ahead, but at least I knew where I was going and why. I was *un*lost.

It had taken me nearly forever not to get *verklempt* when I saw Alex teaching our friend's kids how to skip stones or shoot a basket or make popcorn the old-fashioned way. I satisfied my craving to know what our kids might have been like during extended visits with my two nieces and two nephews. I loved best the opportunity to greet them in the early mornings. With sleepy eyes and pillow-tossed hair they automatically offered up warm hugs. Gold, simply gold. As they tucked into their pancakes or ran around the yard I could see little reminders of Alex and me and our siblings, and I felt a bond – a connection to something much bigger.

CHAPTER NINE

MY INTIMATE REVEAL
AND 15 MINUTES OF FAME

Each day the process of getting more comfortable in my skin became a little easier. One morning I woke up feeling good – strangely good. The feeling was still unfamiliar so it caught me unawares. Could it be because we were heading into a holiday weekend? Alex and I were driving up to the Sierra Nevada Mountains for a getaway. My second thought: *Hey wait a minute, does this feeling of goodness mean I'm getting better?*

Not one to let my feelings go unexplored – a curse if there ever was one – I couldn't understand why it had taken me so long to come to terms with being infertile. Why, I asked myself, had it continued to dog me so? Then an image flashed in my mind. I suddenly saw old Humpty Dumpty coming down off the wall and crashing into a million pieces. Ah, ha! I realized as I reached for my bathrobe – I *am* Humpty Dumpty! When it became evident that the conventional life I had so long envisioned wasn't going to happen, down I came crashing into a million pieces. No king's horses or king's men were going to put me together again. That's because somewhere along the line, after lying there on the ground – for what sometimes felt like *forever* – waiting to be patched up, I'd come to realize that outside help was not coming. I had to figure out how to put myself back together again, and that's what I'd been slowly doing.

I wasn't put back together again nearly as tidy and well-formed as I had been when I was up on the wall. I'm now more of a mosaic – with lots of cracks and mortar and more than a few missing shards. That was the destructive power of not being able to conceive. It was not *just* a medical condition – it was a "bust yourself into a million pieces" condition. I now had to do one better than Humpty Dumpty. I didn't yet know what my life was going to look like, but if mosaics were any indication, they gave me the sense that my life could be beautiful in a different way.

Along with rebuilding myself, I had to rebuild my life – recalibrate my expectations, my relationships, my plans and my future. As John Lennon said, "Life is what happens when you're busy making other plans." A sense of optimism took root and began to flower, nurtured by newfound courage and clarity. Through my writing I systematically began to unlock and express pain I'd bottled up deep inside. I discovered that the final step necessary to drop the shackles that had weighed me down was to apply some of my candor online to my offline world. My silence on the subject clearly had not helped me. To be truly authentic, to rebuild my life unfettered by my clandestine past, I needed to step out of the darkness and acknowledge my infertility and how it had changed me.

My blog had an added benefit. It provided an opening to engage in deeper discussions, in particular with my mother. Until then I had provided her the *Cliffs Notes* version of my infertile life as much to protect her as me. I also provided my mother an early copy of my book manuscript during a visit. A day or so later over a lunch of grilled cheese we talked, tentatively at first, about how much infertility had changed not only my life, but hers as well. Once she realized I was not going to fall apart, she explained how painful it had been to watch me suffer. "I'll never forget the look on your face when your brother's sister-in-law arrived seven months pregnant at Christmas right after … after your last IVF came back negative. I'm your mother. I knew how much you were hurting. Your father, too. He told me how impressed he was with your strength and class."

I choked up as she continued.

"I had to let go of my dreams, too, of sharing in your pregnancy, being on hand to care for you and …"

Infertility clearly caused collateral damage. The losses extended well beyond me.

I also started to forgive those who had wounded me, inadvertently, with their baby and children talk. It was a bit tricky because most didn't even realize they needed to be forgiven. For instance, over lunch I caught up with an old business acquaintance. I tentatively told her about my writing projects and their subject. She couldn't hide her surprise. As I explained the extent of our infertility, she nodded her head. She gently pressed me for more details. I described how beneficial the writing process had been after our IVF proved unsuccessful, how difficult it had been to publicly acknowledge my infertility when her face suddenly went white. She asked when it was that I last underwent IVF.

I cleared my throat; fighting back tears, and told her it had been some four years ago. I said nothing more and went back to eating. She looked off in the distance as though lost in a math equation. She immediately started apologizing. Our last social get-together years ago had started out as a relaxed dinner, a couple's night, less than a month after our final IVF attempt. Still raw in the wake of our embryo loss, whenever I had the strength to socialize it had been, not surprisingly, with couples who didn't have children. We had been well into our appetizers at a boisterous restaurant when they had joyfully shared their news.

"We're expecting!"

It was all I could do then and there not to lose it. I turned to stone. I congratulated them and promptly refilled my wine glass, but the evening proceeded with a completely different tone. I couldn't wait for it to end.

Fast forward to my get-back-in-touch lunch. My intent was never to bring up the difficult dinner and its effects, but my lunch mate suddenly realized that her pregnancy news had collided with my loss. I mistakenly believed enough time had passed, that I had grown tough enough to keep my emotions in check, but the force of the memory came crashing back over our salads. It was as if I were reliving the dinner that very moment, but this time my stony exterior was gone. Tears that I couldn't shed at that past dinner arrived freely this time. (Don't worry; I bring tissues wherever I go now). Much as I tried to discreetly wipe away the tears, it was no use. The waiter was a bit nonplussed when he came to check on our meal. I bowed my head and reached into my purse for another mangled tissue.

My lunch mate got equally emotional. She quietly apologized. We each took a deep breath. She told me she remembered a definite change in my demeanor that night, like a wall had dropped between us but she had no idea why. She'd often wondered, until that point, why I had become so unavailable.

"There's no need to apologize," I tried to reassure her. "How could you be responsible for something you didn't know you were doing?"

That's where my silence hadn't helped me. And that's why I started to come out of the infertility closet. I wasn't leading with the infertility card, but if the opportunity presented itself, I'd make the determination about whether to fill in the blanks. And then something truly wonderful started to happen. A lightness, an effervescence began to return to my life. I wasn't the only one who noticed it. Close friends remarked on it.

I was making peace, too, with Cheerios. Yes. There was a period there when the little beige Os conjured up only images of chubby-cheeked toddlers happily munching away. They, along with a few other things, had been banned or expunged from the house in the infertility days. No longer. Now I was enjoying them again for breakfast – and unlike other Cheerios aficionados I didn't leave a trail of them behind me.

While hanging out intentionally with a pregnant woman might hardly seem worth mentioning to those who don't think twice about it, the odds makers no doubt would have had me down as a long shot. Had I turned the corner? That's what I was wondering when I spent the better part of a weekend socializing with a friend more than halfway through her pregnancy. For me, it was a huge leap forward.

We had gotten together at *my* invitation, although the day I made the offer I had a host of emotionally-charged misgivings. It started when I finally "outed" myself to the woman who had announced her pregnancy earlier in the year at the fortieth birthday party. I tried to dodge her at first, but she and her professor husband had extended numerous invitations to get together. Deep down I knew I needed to get beyond the antisocial state of being "mysteriously" unavailable or I risked a very lonely future. I felt it was safest to reveal myself in an email.

"I want to let you know one of the reasons I've been somewhat preoccupied and hard to reach. I've been dealing with the devastating effects of infertility. I've also been writing a blog about it. I have only disclosed the blog's existence so far to those I trust will be able to treat the content with sensitivity. I hesitated, truthfully, to point it out to you because I don't want to in any way dampen the joy you are experiencing expecting your own child. I'm very happy for you -- especially as you indicated it was taking more time to get pregnant than you expected it might. At the same time I felt that you deserve to know more about a very important part of who I am and why I sometimes seem to withdraw socially. It is not at all personal."

There seemed no better way to reach out to those whom I'd kept at arms length than to gently introduce them to *Coming2Terms*. They could read as much or as little as they wanted on their own time or come back to it when they were ready to contemplate further what it contained. In the meantime I continued to participate in discussions online. I commented on a *New York Times* website post. It concerned a question about a new fertility diet book getting loads of visibility. The question posted to readers: was it help or hype? It spurred quite a debate and provided an opportunity for those who don't cotton much to people with infertility a chance to spew some vitriol. My comment was innocent enough, making the point that fertility was not easily remedied with a diet change and that a little compassion about the experience could go a long way.

A few months later my comment led another *New York Times* reporter to my blog. Her email landed in my inbox with something of a thud. She wanted to know if I'd be willing to participate in an online health feature about infertility. She was trying to gather a representative group of women, the goal being to secure audio clips from five or so of us, discussing our experiences. It had not been easy, she admitted, to locate women willing to acknowledge or discuss, on the record, their infertility. In fact, she'd had a very difficult time finding volunteers. *Why was I not surprised?*

Truthfully, I vacillated. Was I prepared to very publicly divulge my infertile state? Ugh. This should have been a fairly easy decision, right? After all, wasn't I pounding the table demanding an end to the stigma associated with not being able to conceive? Yeah, well, it was one thing to reveal my blog to trusted friends and family; it was quite another to announce my very personal struggle to the world at large. At the same time I knew with more than one hundred blog posts searchable online, it would be hard to keep such a thing secret for forever. In fact, I wrote each entry with the idea that *Coming2Terms* would one day be linked to me by anyone who took the time to connect the dots. My clues were easy enough to follow. This didn't require the characters from *CSI* to crack the case. Was I prepared to seize this opportunity? To set an example on a larger stage? It was now or never. Forever hide in the shadows or step into the light. I hemmed and hawed while her email sat in my inbox. Realizing I had to walk the talk or suffer the consequences, I agreed to participate.

So, when was the last time you read a story about an infertile couple that wasn't just a tad freaky – especially if an entire family was delivered all in one day, or heard the one about an anguished infertile, desperate to fill a void, kidnapping a baby? Yeah, I figured as much. Well I wanted nothing more than to be the exception rather than the rule. I can be non-neurotic, sane as the next guy when I work at it. The reporter and I talked and taped my segment in April, but the piece wouldn't run until June, just days ahead of my forty-fifth birthday.

But first I had another Mother's Day to survive. No matter how old I got, in the eyes of my father I would always be an innocent, once cross-eyed little girl who needed to be safeguarded. While my dad is not as physically strong as he once was, he is still there to slay my dragons, look out for my best interests and keep me from harm. Our best visits are now in the early morning when he's well-rested. That's when the damage from a series of strokes that left him searching for words from his once vibrant vocabulary seemed the least obvious. I found him on the second Sunday morning in May watching Katherine Hepburn and Spencer Tracy in *Desk Set*. I curled up on the sofa cushion next to him.

"Pambo, have you seen this movie? Her character reminds me of you."

I shook my head no and we spent the next hour laughing and enjoying the witty dialogue. During commercial breaks we compared headlines from *The New York Times*. Not a word was said about it being Mother's Day. We had taken my mother out for a celebratory lunch some twenty-four hours before the full onslaught of mommydom, on account of my flight departing at noon.

An hour later I was dressed and dropping him by the church at the end of our street. Despite his stroke he could, thankfully, still sing. He has a beautiful voice. The choir assembled early so my mother would join him later. We pulled up to the curb. I got out of the car to say my good-byes, and I was secretly grateful that I wouldn't have to go inside with him. In the last few minutes of our visit together, he grabbed my hand and said haltingly, "You know, this is the Mass where they have that awful display. When they ask all the mothers to stand. And all I can do is think of you and those like you and ..."

His eyes teared up. My eyes teared up. Neither of us knew what to say next. And then I became a little girl again. I fell into his arms for a hug. He held me tightly and whispered in my ear, "Goodbye, baby."

I watched as he made his way down the church steps and I had a good cry. I had been able to avoid the annual mama-palooza and the excruciating experience of sitting in church while all the women around me stood to be blessed, but I couldn't avoid the wave of emotions that the day inevitably brought forth. I'm just glad my dad was there to help make it all better.

Turning forty-five presented a new reason to stand back and assess my life. I would officially be outside the statistical window of childbearing years: fifteen to forty-four. Strange, I know, but the age boundary offered a certain peace of mind. Meanwhile *The New York Times* reporter followed up and told me my comments from the audio segment had provoked interest in a larger feature piece on infertility for the print edition. This led to a nail-biting wait of a different kind. What had started as an online health piece contained deep inside the very complex *New York Times* website would now have a companion print piece – easily read by anyone in an airport or coffee shop. What I didn't fully appreciate was that the print piece would be a feature solely about me and Alex.

It got even more surreal. One of my bloggie friends emailed me the afternoon on the day the story was out suggesting that I might want to check out *The New York Times* home page. I clicked over expecting to see a link to the audio health segment. When the site loaded I found a picture of me staring back from the home page. I WAS ON THE HOME-PAGE OF THE FREAKIN' NEW YORK TIMES! The central photo was usually reserved for heads of state or natural disasters. But for one hour on June 10, 2008 there I was: Pamela Mahoney Tsigdinos (a natural disaster of another sort, perhaps?) taking ownership of her infertility with the headline: "After Years of Fertility Treatments: Facing Life Without Children." Ironically, one of the other headlines further below my picture and caption read: "Operation Lets Muslim Women Reclaim Virginity." The universe sure has a twisted sense of humor. There were some choice – okay, seriously heartless – comments left in response:

> "I have little sympathy for people who can't have their own children. No one ever promised you a rose garden, and no one ever promised you a perfect family, either. Sometimes, you need to suck it up..."

> "Where do you draw the line between other's insensitivity and the infertile couple's selfishness?"

> "Do infertility patients really rate the same sympathy as those suffering debilitating, painful or lethal diseases? That's essentially the claim - we're suffering just as much as they are. I don't think so. You're not even suffering as much as someone who lost a limb, since you haven't lost something you had and which was intrinsic to you, you've lost merely

the opportunity to perpetuate your genes (a biological instinct which rationality ought to be able to overcome) and
the ability to have the next in the series of lifestyle choices
(parenthood)."

"Such folks don't long to 'parent'. What they long for is to fit
in (and compete) with their white suburban neighbors and
produce yet another 'mini-me'".

I didn't take their comments personally. Actually, I felt kind of sorry
for the people who left them. It must suck to be so mean-spirited or to
embody what someone once described as blatant "compassion fatigue."
Furthermore, my skin had gotten quite thick over the years – a far cry
from the days when it felt like I had no skin at all, when every careless
comment caused lasting suffering. There were more than a few supportive comments, too, from places far and wide. That's because the story also
ran in the *International Herald Tribune* and was picked up in newspapers
as far away as Brazil, Poland and Nigeria. One of the most gutt-wrench-
ing comments came from an African woman who wrote:

"Married for years without any child. It's been an emotional
roller coaster for the both of us due to family, cultural &
social pressure. Not been informed about pregnancies and
births cuz we don't have a child of ours. At first I ignored it
but it hurts deeply. I have lost friendships cuz of this 'stigma.'
Every month when I see my period my heart tears apart. I
pressured my husband for us to seek medical help and that's
when we discovered that he has NO SPERM, my gosh it was
a terrible day hearing that information, most especially when
we tried IVF & it failed. It was the worst day of my Life."

While the article didn't lead to an overnight change in attitudes, as with
any topic shrouded in taboo, we had to start somewhere, right? It was one
in what I hope will continue to be a series of -- what do they call them in

school today — teachable moments? The act of coming out of the darkness also allowed me to feel whole again. More women and men around the world found my blog. They filled my inbox with thank you notes for having the guts to speak up. They told me they felt less alone. Equally satisfying were the emails and comments I received from those who were *not* infertile. The vast majority overflowed with compassion and kindness:

> "I learned about your blog from the NYT. Thank you for the courage, humor, and honesty that you so openly share with other women. I went to it for other reasons than infertility though. A best girlfriend of mine - we've known each other since we were 13 - was going through a lot trying to get pregnant. When her trials started, she distanced herself from her friends. She has always been a private person, so I suspected that she was going through a lot and I didn't want to pry and wanted to respect her privacy. However, I wanted to be a good friend and remain open enough, hoping that she would open up to me one day, on her terms, with her comfort level. But she never even said the word 'boo' about trying to conceive - good, bad, or ugly. When I became pregnant (rather quickly, despite many doctors telling me otherwise) our friendship virtually vanished. I felt guilty and sad, but I could not hide my "fertile" self. I've wanted to be able to understand what she was going through, to help shoulder some worry. To know how to act, to understand her sensitivities, but there was a big wall there, so I couldn't. Your blog has helped me understand a little better. So you are not only helping women and couples who are infertile, but friendships among women too. Thank you. All the best to you."

> "I read your courageous article in the *New York Times*. I want to congratulate you on bringing this issue into the

light. You are a role model for many women. I totally iden-
tify with your analogy of accepting your loss as I have had to
learn to live with two very different losses around the similar issues: motherhood. I was one of thousands of women
who lost a child to adoption. Like many of the 'Girls Who
Went Away' many women then and still today - experience
this loss NOT BY CHOICE but because of lack of options
and choices. Our choices are taken from us not by physical
circumstances, but social mores, others' concerns, poverty,
etc. Like you, we deal with the pain of our loss daily and
it is especially acute on birthdays, anniversaries, Mother's
Day etc. Like you - we deal with shame, grief, loss and pain
that is often NOT understood. In fact, we are often con-
fronted with very negative, cruel, judgmental comments.
I've actually heard 'any dog can give birth'! We are made to
feel like societal lepers. The only solution I have and others
have found is to face and channel the anger constructively,
like the mothers who turned their loss into MADD! Working to help others deal with their loss, being there hand-
holding...AND, like you, enlightening the public and trying
to change social attitudes! Adoption is NOT a solution for
infertility. All too often it is seen as just the 'next step' in
infertility 'treatments' as if taking someone else's child and
causing them pain and loss will somehow cure yours. That
is most unfair to children who are made to feel like 'replace-
ments.' Continue to speak out!"

"You are very brave to share your story of infertility in the
NYTimes article and in your blog. I'm a 10+ year veteran of
infertility treatment, and appreciate your candidness in the
article. Although my husband and I have shared parts of our
story with a few people, we have never done this in a very
public way. Your story was deeply moving to me. I'm sorry

you and the other participants in the article were subjected
to some of the insensitive, ignorant comments the article received. Please know that your openness helps give strength
to other infertile people and helps educate those who want
to be educated."

These and other emails and comments touched my heart – almost
filling up the hole that had been created following our losses. Collectively
they erased a world of hurt. I never expected my fifteen minutes of fame
would be quite so, well, personal (the piece showed line drawings meant
to be my uterus and Alex's private parts after all) but it felt good not to be
in hiding any more, a nameless, faceless infertility data point or statistic.
By stepping forward, along with the five other women who provided their
perspective in the audio segment, we provided a view into what it was like
for an infertile person to combat nature, and then when that didn't work,
to try to make our way in a fertile world oblivious to our pain.

The multi-media feature helped reveal that infertility is about much
more than the act of creating a baby. It is a condition, an experience that
impacts a lifetime. It's near impossible to pretend away major life milestones when everyone around you is talking about them, living them. And
layer on top of that a pervasive societal insensitivity about what's involved
in recovering from such an experience -- "So, you couldn't have kids, yeah,
well whatever! Have I told you how great mine are? I haaaavvvve PIC-
TURES!" -- and there are bound to be setbacks and painful reminders.

CHAPTER TEN

A NEW BEGINNING: A REBIRTH
OF ANOTHER SORT

Through my blog and in my "second life," I had been transported back to my younger days before the world first subdivided – peeling off into the dating or not-dating crowd, followed by the married or not-married subdivision ... then pregnant, not-pregnant, only to lead to the mommy, not-mommy separation. In the blogosphere I had been able to relate deeply once again with other women, and experience a connection that had been missing in my life. I was in a state of nirvana – for a while that is. Life doesn't stand still even when we want it to. There I was letting my hair down and grooving with the infertile gals in bloggie land, when a different sort of sucker punch landed. My infertile pals started falling pregnant.

I don't know why it surprised me. They were, after all, mostly in various stages of extreme treatment. Their pregnancy inhibitors varied widely, some more treatable then others. It was inevitable that the hormone shots and embryo transfers sooner or later would work for some of them. But you want to talk feeling really infertile – *bona fide* barren? I was transported again to earlier days, but this time I was reliving what it felt like to sit by idly while women showed off their first trimester ultrasound photos. Only this time, online, it was weirder. You see, there's a "decoration" that can be added to a blog sidebar. It's ghoulish and surreal, a dynamic illustration of a fetus developing in a womb. Yes, it actually mirrored the real deal, changing day by day with the days since conception included. I kid you not.

That wasn't all. Some women exhibited the same behaviors they had only months earlier decried in other women, writing about which food induced the worst nausea, including cropped photos of themselves with their now swelling bellies. It felt like a new adaptation of *Invasion of the Body Snatchers*. Bizarre, really. I wasn't fully prepared for the same "wonders of pregnancy" behaviors from women who were only days and weeks earlier, pre-pregnancy, just like me. In fairness, not all my infertile friends crossed over to the prega-palooza side. Some just stopped blogging, deciding it was too cruel to chronicle their pregnancies in such an overt way. They saw it as the equivalent of complaining about a bountiful harvest to those having to make do in drought-stricken regions. Others started companion blogs for the blow-by-blow during the forty-week wait while they continued to write about the impact of infertility after pregnancy – on the way they approached baby showers and the residual trauma and flashbacks caused by visits to the doctor's office.

With the panoply of pregnancies taking place all over my blogroll, I realized I would have to adjust, learn to cope with the sense of being on the outside looking in yet again. (It's okay. I was getting pretty good at it.) Just as in real life, my virtual friends were peeling off into new directions. Some of the intensely personal relationships, sadly, often were fleeting ones. Sure there were new women logging on every day for the first time, but it's not emotionally healthy to live in a permanent state of trying to conceive (TTC) drama-rama. Just as I didn't want to add any more new moms to my real life social life, I was less interested in forming new relationships online with women just entering the infertility arena. I felt like a senior facing graduation day when the new class of wide-eyed freshmen showed up on campus. I wished them well, but we were at two different points in our lives. They wanted to commune with their incoming TTC classmates.

The younger infertile bloggers had the full benefit of camaraderie, time and options in ways that I never had at the same age. Those in their twenties and thirties could gather information and insights more efficiently than ever before. They literally could tap into the wisdom of crowds without leaving their homes. In a safe cocoon they could anonymously sample and explore complex ideas and emotions 24/7. A 3:00 a.m. pajama fit because they were worried about the drugs they were on? No problem, log onto the Internet. Feeling isolated and need to vent? No worries, Cinderella125girl in Australia might be online. It was remarkable, really, to have such an extraordinary support and information network at the ready.

At the same time I had to reconcile all the new fertility-related information now available. Hardly a week went by when there wasn't some new study talking about a promising new fertility discovery or a way to combat a nefarious contributor to infertility. For instance, there were two studies back to back, one about the 350 genes involved in female fertility and another about the impact of soy on sperm. It wasn't so long ago that I would have devoured those stories. I would have feasted on the potential for the next study to provide the miraculous formula necessary to get me knocked up. And mainstream news? When random fertility-related headlines splashed across online or TV news I approached them with trepidation. Sometimes, depending on my mood, I avoided them altogether. I knew full well there would likely come a day when a massive scientific breakthrough would occur on the fertility front. The promise associated with freezing eggs, for instance, gets more real all the time. And I also know that it will be too late for me. (*Cue the violins.*)

I raise this because I often wonder how women who experienced infertility issues in their prime-time mommy years in, say, the 1950s, 1960s or even 1970s perceived IUIs and IVFs when they came screaming on the scene to jumpstart conception and pregnancy. How did it feel for them to see their younger sisters succeed where they hadn't, after their window of opportunity had closed? Envy is certainly something they must have experienced, but to know that if the development had just come earlier they might have succeeded themselves – that had to be hard, like being the last person to be diagnosed with polio just weeks *before* the vaccine became available.

So, in this seemingly never-ending journey of making adjustments and trying to find ways to cope with pregnancies – and all that came with them – I saw I had more to learn. How would I have been if I had ever succeeded in getting a bun in the oven? I honestly don't know. That's why I'm not passing judgment on my newly-pregnant infertile online associates. I just don't know if I would have been any different. What's more, I'll never know.

While more than a few of my online pals were getting pregnant, still others had worked through their grief and elected to pursue adoption – open, closed, domestic, international, etc. – or they were on the path to donor eggs/sperm or surrogacy. The blog authors clustered around their various subtopics. Each path to parenthood had its own protocols and expenses and time lines. I looked around and realized I had an example of my own to set. Through blogging infertility I had been making up for the years when I had no cohorts whom I could relate to. I might have been *biologically* into my forties when I entered the blogosphere, but *emotionally* I was in my mid-thirties. It was cathartic at first to converse online (and, yes, rant when needed about how hard it could be to tolerate certain naturally-occurring moms), but once I'd said and heard just about everything there was to say about my experience, I started to feel my age in a different sort of way. I was ready to graduate from what had amounted to remedial infertility.

The vast majority of infertility blogs, like life itself, are about the journey to somewhere and the decisions that need to be made along the way. After the decisions are made you'd typically arrive at your destination and, in time, a new road map would have to be drawn up. What about the women like me who decided enough was enough on the medical front, but that adoption or donor eggs or sperm didn't feel right either? Some stopped blogging entirely. Others recast their blogs into broader topics that didn't focus exclusively on infertility. I was one of a handful of women, *the post-infertility trauma edition* types, writing about what happened once the childbearing dreams had been set free. It was as if I were six years old again sitting astride my banana seat in the driveway wondering what it would be like to ride, but fearful about the lumps, scrapes and bruises awaiting me.

With each day I got better at finding my balance, learning how to avoid the equivalent of cement parking blocks. I was also not alone. I had what amounted to a *peloton* – strong women riding along with me.

When I wasn't blogging from our kitchen in my free time, Alex and I turned our attention to the state of our house. It had been one of the casualties of infertility. It was a modest-sized but quirky ranch. We had bought it in the early days of fertility treatment in part because it was located in one of the best school districts in the Bay area. The house, though, was confused. It didn't know if it wanted to be 1968 California ranch with three tiny bedrooms, or a 1979 groovy pad with track lighting and a European kitchen that opened into a large solarium – compliments of a previous owner who clearly had visions of a party house. The backyard held a forty-year-old in-ground pool with an ancient, wheezing gas heater that we rarely turned on, since it cost a fortune to take the chill out of the water. We pretended that our pool was really a brisk freshwater lake – like Torch Lake in northern Michigan, which will turn your lips blue in August. We had had fragile dreams of turning one of the three bedrooms into a nursery, of one day playing in the pool with our kid(s), and of having noisy coloring contests in the sun-splashed kitchen.

Those were the days when we didn't spend a dime on the house because we put all of our money into doctor visits and treatments. Our house stayed confused with kitchen appliances that threatened regularly to die. We nursed our dishwasher along, joked about putting our refrigerator into the Smithsonian, and watched as our stovetop went from four to two functioning burners. One day our stove vent just stopped working. I think it went on strike in solidarity with my uterus. We looked into replacing the built-in stove, but it was a complicated architecture and would require tearing up part of the kitchen. In time, our white cabinets took on a yellowed look from the steam generated from one too many pots of boiling pasta.

The question became: if we're even going to touch the kitchen, and we're going to get new appliances and cabinets, why don't we just re-do the kitchen entirely and bring it into the twenty-first century? Meanwhile, the pool hadn't been getting much use but we were constantly refilling it at a time when California was in a semi-drought. If we filled it in we'd have room to expand the little bedroom we inhabited and put in a roomy master suite. We carefully mapped out a new house plan with an architect and hired a contractor. Before long the disruptive work began.

In particular, it was disturbing and surreal to see the pool go away. It was a burial in every sense of the word. Each day a crew came adding and compacting more dirt. In watching the process I felt my stomach clench. Tears burned in my eyes. There would be no swim diapers, no cannon-balls from the diving board now gone, and no laughter coming from the backyard. I knew, *intellectually*, while the pool existed we wouldn't have any children to share it with, but seeing it removed before my very eyes brought the reality home in a visceral way. I'm glad it's now gone entirely, buried along with my dreams.

As the remodel slowly evolved, weirdly, I found myself pregnant with anticipation. Each day there were tangible changes, incontrovert-ible progress. The drywall went in and the rough plumbing appeared. I walked into the new rooms without any flooring and imagined a new future – no longer haunted by the dreams of the old one. A new life took shape, one that could be both barren and beautiful – two words not nor-mally joined together. I regained the sense of being a woman-child, much as when my world first turned Technicolor. But now, some twenty-five years later, I had to recast the narrative of my life and with it my earliest formed beliefs:

- Steer clear of marriage where there's no power-sharing agree-ment and make sure your mate is compatible. **Check.**

- The world is my oyster. I can still grow up to be anything I want to be. **Check.**

- Don't confuse "fitting in" with being successful. **Check.**

- Be aware that kids are ~~a big responsibility so make sure you're ready for them~~ not a given and that your inability to conceive and deliver them doesn't mean your life will lack meaning or legacy. (*Warning: If you're a "fertile" person don't even think about saying this to someone in the throes of battling infertility – you could get seriously hurt! Remember, only we who have made the rocky journey that got us to the mountain top can make that statement without looking disingenuous.)*

There is the residue of an experience in life that continues to shape us long after the actual experience has ended. We stretch and grow and learn a lot while living through it. Then we learn a little more after we've had some distance. We carry from such experiences indelible memories and, if it was a particularly bad experience, there's usually some unfinished business.

In my case, and for others in my shoes, I suspect the business of sorting out the emotions, conflicts and what ifs will continue. I likely have a few infertility hairballs left to expel. The sorting process is inevitable as we infertiles make our ways in life, and see our more fertile family and friends take on the role of mother- or father-of-the-bride or groom and then, if they're fortunate, become grandparents. But I am no longer afraid of my infertility demons. The pain they inflicted has dulled and the scars have begun to fade. I'm no longer on the lookout for places to hide.

And the fear of failure? *Fuhgettaboutit!* Bring on the challenges, because once you've overcome a failure that has rocked you to your core there's very little else that seems imposing by comparison. Will there be "pregnant pauses" in my future when new acquaintances ask, as they inevitably will, if we have children? Without a doubt. What will I answer? It will depend on the circumstances. A few answers I've been dying to use – and they're sure to get a few confused stares: "Children? What a funny question. Can't you see I've evolved to perfection?" Or "There's so much more to that question than we have time for now. Read this book called *Silent Sorority* – you can get it online. Let's have a nice long chat when you're through with it. Now, where *are* those appetizers? I'm starving…"

Meanwhile, it took a 2,400 mile trip back home one long weekend, in the bedroom where I once spun buoyant, cotton candy plans for my future, to make me see how I had spent the better part of my adulthood chasing the sort of life that was never meant be. It wasn't easy to recognize that the pattern I cut never did quite fit – much like the blue jean overalls misfire from my Home Economics class. I was fourteen then, and like most girls in my junior high school I took a Home Ec class that included learning to sew. The final class project involved a fashion show where the class of girls (no boy would be caught dead taking Home Ec) would model their creations. I worked for a semester on those blue jean overalls. I wanted so badly to have a pair hanging in my closet. I was determined to get it right. I combed through bolts of fabric to find the right denim material. I scrutinized the complex sewing pattern to make sure I knew how to get from raw material to finished product. Ever so carefully I measured and cut the tissue pattern. I pinned it in place, held my breath and began to cut.

I engaged in what felt like epic battles with the sewing machine. Sometimes it won, and I had to remove the thread to start the bib or the leg all over again to get the seams straight. Finally I stitched the last stitch. I triumphantly carried my new outfit home. As I went upstairs to my bedroom to try the overalls on for the first time my mind filled with thoughts about how I'd look in the fashion show. Only the images in my mind didn't align with what stared back at me from the mirror. I had grown at least two inches since the class had begun, on my way to six feet tall. My blue jean overalls turned out to look like the worst fashion faux pas of junior high school. I was wearing flood pants. I blushed my way through the fashion show and never wore the overalls again.

My father's metaphor about life as a smorgasbord came back to me as I stood looking in the mirror trying to find evidence of the girl who was once eager to sample all life had to offer. It seemed I'd tasted far too many bitter, heartburn-causing dishes in recent years. Surely there had to be more variety – a life that was a little more free range, one less dictated by someone else's menu or norms. Those thoughts, in turn, reminded me of Alex's epiphany in Germany about what is, in fact, *our* normal.

Epiphanies don't come every day but when they do they feel so obvious. I relished the moment. The experience of looking ahead and not back was oddly familiar, a *déjà vu* moment. There was something so recognizable. What *was* it? Hang on. Is that my old friend, Hope? Where the *hell* have you been hiding anyway? Look, I'm so done with trying to wear the equivalent of flood pants and feeling all conspicuous for not being like everyone else. This body may be barren but that doesn't mean it can't do other things. The predictably, happily-ever-after ending is overrated. Give me an independent film ending any day. Maybe Alex and I will travel the world, stay in yurts, indulge in our fascination with history and help bring new stories to life. Maybe we will get carbon credits for creating a smaller footprint on the planet as a family of two.

My rebirth and re-acquaintance with hope felt invigorating. After a long time wandering alone in the proverbial desert picking up shards of glass and tile to create my mosaic I finally could say with some gusto, *screw* the minivan! Outside of my blog I labored on this manuscript. I wanted to help shape a world where girls (and boys) who might, unfortunately, grow up and face fertility problems didn't find themselves on the receiving end of sentiments like one search query that brought someone to my blog: **how to get your barren friend to stop being a weird bitch.**

Oh, no, you di'int!

Seriously – you want to talk red meat potential? I could take the bait or go off like a Roman candle, but instead I'll say to the person who entered the query:

> Your friend is *not* weird and she's no bitch either if you consider what it's like to be in her skin. Imagine walking through what amounts to quicksand with "friends" like you refusing to toss out a lifeline. Now about your own plans to conceive – do you really think your mean genes have earned the right to be passed along? The world has more than enough of your kind. Hey, but there's hope for you yet. There's this woman in the Midwest I'd like you to meet. She can be found sitting down in church on Mother's Day.

EPILOGUE

While many people rely on their children to bring new experiences into their lives, to see the world anew, what I've learned is that we each have the capacity to make new discoveries about ourselves and others if we keep our eyes and minds open. Election night 2008 was unlike any I'd ever witnessed. I was struck by the moments of graciousness, the oneness, the powerful coming together of past and future. I admired Senator John McCain's concession speech, his encouragement "to bridge our differences." I was equally impressed with [then] Senator Barack Obama's call to "a new spirit of patriotism; of service and responsibility where each of us resolves to pitch in and work harder and look after not only ourselves, but each other."A defining moment in history to be sure. As uplifted as I was by the rhetoric and pageantry, I had more than one or two pangs of envy when I heard talk of one day reliving the moment with grandchildren. No election would be complete if politicians and pundits didn't talk repeatedly about the importance of leaving the world a better place for "our children" or ensuring that we create abundant opportunities and options for "future generations."

While intellectually I agree wholeheartedly with the sentiments, those expressions also chafed some. It was one thing to know deep down that infertility robbed us of many life-defining experiences, and it was quite another to be reminded (repeatedly) that a whole host of experiences will never get passed along. So, what did I do to overcome those pangs and chafes? I reminded myself that we are all in this together, that "our children" is a collective term. That night taught me again that there is no more powerful feeling than being a part of something greater than ourselves.

I no longer obsess about lists and control. I've come to embrace ambiguity. I hope that in speaking out about infertility other couples will feel less isolated in their experience. As this email from a blog reader showed me, the ability to touch and help someone else is not solely the province of mothers and fathers:

> "We gave up trying to get pregnant via medical help over a year ago, and though I have spent hours over months over years searching the Internet for any help that might be out there (even emotional, to deal with the loss infertility has brought to our lives), I have never come across the perspective of someone who's accepted a childless life. For whatever reason, we are not (and I don't believe we will be) able to emotionally consider adoption. I do wonder what it will be like to live without my life-long dream, and I am trying to ready myself. Thank you for sharing your thoughts as you have 'moved on' with your life. I suspected the pain would never go away, really. I have slowly changed as my fruitless struggle to conceive has endured... my sister said I'm not who I used to be before this experience. I can feel it... Anyway, thank you."

THE SORORITY SPEAKS

I've had thousands of comments logged on my blog or sent as emails by those at various stages of confronting infertility. Here are some thoughts, bits and pieces of advice, left by readers for their more "fertile" counterparts:

- "Be a little more observant about those who don't seem to have children or don't talk about children. We get that you are proud and excited about your children, but please try to tune in and see if your listener gets a pained look or if their eyes glaze over when you talk about your little ones. Chances are very, very good that we – and those who are childfree by choice for that matter – don't want to hear all about your children and the trials, joys and challenges of being a parent, the cost of daycare, tuition, or toys. It's not that we don't care... it's just that, well, sometimes that's all you want talk about and we have little or nothing to add to the conversation."

- "Let's talk mass emails for birth announcements. They are *so* wrong especially when they're sent out willy-nilly to the entire workplace (complete with birth stats and labor and delivery room photos)."

- "Remember, not everyone has children and more than likely we may not want to be reminded of that fact in such a blatant unexpected way. Happily, there are lots of other topics we can discuss in person or via email: sports, politics, movies, books, interest rates, travel, cars, hobbies, and, of course, the old standby: weather. The best bet is, if you know or suspect you're in the presence of an infertile, let her start the conversation about the kids – if we bring it up, feel free to go for it. We're probably having a really good day."

- "I'd like fertile people to understand that the disappointment they may have felt if they tried to conceive for several months before having success is NOT the same as the devastation of being diagnosed as infertile. By the by, one other thing to avoid saying: "it was God's Will." That's the equivalent of saying that God wanted you to have a baby, but not us - that God doesn't see us as fit to be bear a child."

- "You should never, never ask a woman when/if she's going to have kids. If she's already been trying for a while, it will feel like a knife to the heart. It forces her to either tell you more than she wanted to or to lie. Because if she had wanted to talk about having kids in the first place, she would have."

- "That asking us to admire their babies, hold them, babysit even, is NOT a cure for our wounded hearts but more akin to rubbing our faces in our loss. Seriously, mothers, stop it. It isn't funny, kind, or cute. It isn't compassionate. Your beautiful child doesn't 'make up' for our lack of children. If we love you, and love your children, we will forge our own loving, close relationship with them, in our own time. Stop shoving."

- "That telling a woman who has lost a baby that 'it wasn't meant to be' is not compassionate. It's merely a way of easing your own discomfort by dismissing ours. Ditto not mentioning our losses to us. That minimizing our pain, be it through offering "solutions" or explanations only serves to make yourself feel better while inflicting further hurt on us. They are free to do that, of course, but they have to understand that we may, as a result, see them as emotionally stunted and extremely self-absorbed twits. Yes, it's hard to contemplate the randomness of the cruel universe where bad things happen to good people, and it may make it easier for them to sleep if they can convince themselves that there is a reason for all of it, and we must've deserved it. But they might want to consider how hard it is being the one to whom bad shit happens. And they might want to maybe try not adding to the hurt by dismissing it. That telling us you know what we're going through because it took you X months to get pg minimizes our feelings. You had a happy ending - we may not. That's not us being negative – it's us being realistic. That telling us to take your kids for the weekend will "cure us" of wanting children is infuriating. Not only are you rubbing in what we don't have — you've basically just told us that you don't really want it either."

- "STOP PUTTING PICTURES ON FACEBOOK, AN-NOUNCING TO THE WHOLE WORLD THAT YOUR BABY IS 1MTH OLD, 2MTH OLD, 3MTH OLD. When will the announcement stop? Till he/she reaches 21????? It's so annoying because that's a constant reminder to me how time flies and yet I am NOT a mother."

- "Please stop assuming that because I have no children I know nothing about parenting."

- "That you (as a fertile person) can never make the hurt go away, but you CAN take steps to not rub it in my face. So don't complain to me. They should assume we are happy for them, but also having difficulty dealing with the news."

- "Schoolteachers do not consider teaching a substitute for parenting, and that our students are not our surrogate children. Blech. I am quite capable of distinguishing between the role of teacher and the role of parent. There's great value in sitting, listening and sympathizing. No judging, no fixing. Not even any understanding, necessarily, because that's an impossible task. Just being and hearing."

- "One of the things that has been coming up for me lately has been the metaphorical process of giving birth to myself. I've been stripped down and made new in this journey, I've become utterly vulnerable, and I feel as though I've been forced to see the world differently. Maybe this is my way to try to find meaning in everything, and perhaps it's grasping a bit too much. But I am a different person than I was before. In some ways, it's because I have had to truly confront and accept that things don't always go as I planned or as I wished. There is disappointment in life, and I have to live with that. I'm going to have to live with the decisions I've made along the way, and if I'm lucky enough to have children, they are going to have to live with those decisions, too. I can be somewhat at peace, reminding myself that things are as they are. But I'll never have the kind of optimism that some people have that anything is possible, that it will all work out in the end (of course it does, it's just sometimes massively devastating, which is one outcome that is often overlooked by those who've never really been dealt the kind of disappointment one has to face in infertility."

- "In dealing with infertility, I have had to take responsibility for my life and my choices in a deeper way than I ever had before. And because we live in a society where so few seem to take true responsibility for themselves and for those around them, it is very lonely. We don't live in a world that really embraces soul-searching, and so much of this journey has been about soul-searching for me. I think a lot of the assvice [bad or unsolicited advice] and glib responses to infertility (like "just adopt" or "it wasn't meant to be") are because people are so uncomfortable with pain and the possibility of pain with no resolution. They think it's fixable - it has to be, right, with enough money and technology and prayer and intention and positive thinking?! The truth is that it's not fixable. Even though we are strong enough to live through it, to re-create ourselves, to give birth to new lives for ourselves. We can't take away the pain. All we can do is transform in response to it."

ACKNOWLEDGEMENTS

This book would not have been possible without the loving support, patience and involvement of my family and especially my husband Alex. Many others reviewed multiple drafts and provided invaluable support and encouragement: Susan Fallon; Catherine Derr; Julie Kleis-Bramer; Teresa O'Kane; Gail Pomerantz; Jane Lang; Dawn Miller; Angela Parsons; Irene Prokop; Ellen Kunkelmann; Norri Kageki; Melissa Ford; Melissa L. Owsley; Kimberly Pryor; Kelly Damron; Lori Dowd; Petra Dierkes-Thrun; Jill Balin Rembar; Wendy Rogers; Christina Gombar; and Andrea Chapin. I'd also like to thank my fellow bloggers and the thousands of *Coming2Terms* readers who have left comments. All were instrumental in helping me come to terms with my infertility experience, and heal. There is no greater gift to offer those coping with this experience than compassion.

RESOURCES

American Society of Reproductive Medicine: www.asrm.org

Centers for Disease Control and Prevention:
www.cdc.gov/ART/index.htm

Fertility Authority: www.fertilityauthority.com

Infertility Awareness Association of Canada: www.iaac.ca

International Council on Infertility Information Dissemination:
www.inciid.org

International Premature Ovarian Failure Association:
www.pofsupport.org

More to Life Support for the Involuntarily Childless:
www.infertilitynetwork.uk.com

RESOLVE: The National Infertility Association: www.resolve.org

The Finnish Infertility Association (Simpukka)
www.simpukka.info/fi_fi/briefly-in-english

Women's Health.gov: www.womenshealth.gov/faq/infertility.cfm

Made in the USA
Charleston, SC
16 March 2011